# Sailors of the Sky

*Published by*

Sebastian Press
Western American Diocese of the Serbian Orthodox Church

**Contemporary Christian Thought Series, number 7**

First Edition.

*Prepress & printing*
Interklima-grafika, Vrnjci, Srbija

*Address all correspondence to:*
Sebastian Press
1621 West Garvey Avenue
Alhambra, California 91803

E-mail: info@westsrbdio.org ❖ Website: http://www.westsrbdio.org

Publishers Cataloging-in-Publication

Bigović, Fr. Radovan.
    Sailors of the sky : a conversation with Fr. Stamatis Skliris and Fr. Marko
    Rupnik on contemporary Christian art / by Fr. Radovan Bigovic ;
    afterword by Bishop Maxim of Western America ; translated from Serbian
    by Ivana Jakovljevic, Fr. Gregory Edwards and Andrijana Krstic.—1st
    ed.—Alhambra, Calif. : Sebastian Press/Western American Diocese of the
    Serbian Orthodox Church, 2010.
        96 p. ; 23 cm.
        (Contemporary Christian thought series; no. 7)
        ISBN: 978-0-9719505-8-0
        1. Christianity and art—Orthodox Eastern Church. 2. Christian
    art and symbolism. 3. Icons. 4. Art, Modern. 5. Orthodox Eastern
    Church—Doctrines. I. Sklērēs, Stamatēs. II. Rupnik, Marko Ivan, 1954–
    III. Title. IV. Series.

N8187.B54 2010                        2010929471
704.9/482—dc22                1 0 0 6

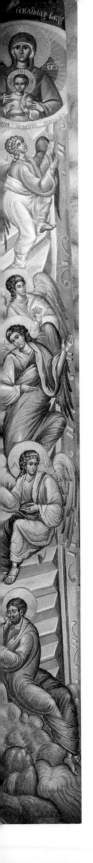
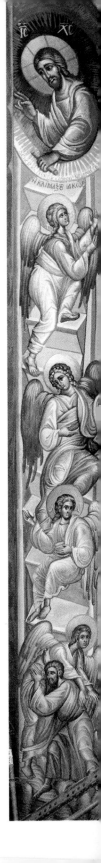

# Sailors of the Sky

A conversation with
**Fr. Stamatis Skliris**
and
**Fr. Marko Rupnik**
on contemporary Christian art

**by Fr. Radovan Bigovic**

**Afterword by Bishop Maxim
of Western America**

Translated from Serbian by
Ivana Jakovljevic, Fr. Gregory Edwards
and Andrijana Krstic

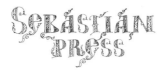

2010

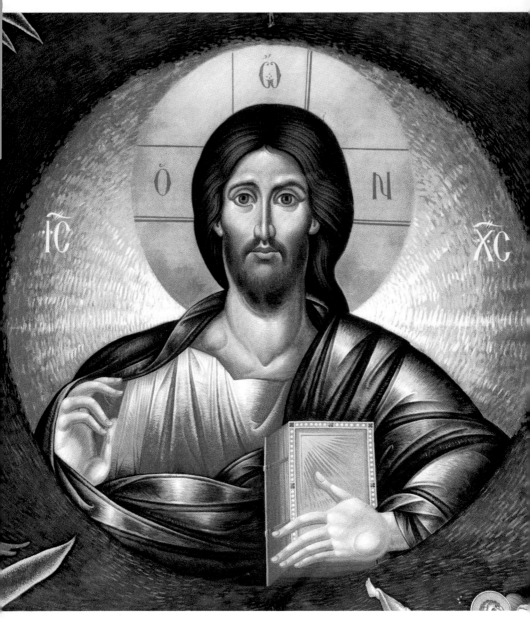

*Stamatis Skliris*
**Christ Pantocrator,**
acrylic on canvas,
Church of the Holy Prophet Elijah,
Castela-Piraeus, 2001

*1. What is the role of art in the life
of the Church today?*

**Fr. Marko:** Art was always of great importance in the
life of the Church. Today, its role and position in the
Church are becoming even more important because,
in the past few centuries, thought has started to
move toward a more abstract and theoretical,
philosophical approach. It is very dangerous to think
of Christianity as an ideology among many others, as
one of many moral theories. This is not only
threatening the Western church, because I have often
gotten the impression, in listening to sermons of
Orthodox priests, that moralism has become a
problem among Eastern Christians, too.

It appears, then, to be urgently necessary for us to
establish and put into practice the principle that
what can be said can also be seen – that is, to unify
word and image. Christ is the Word, He is the Logos,
but the Logos is the Son of God, a Person. The
Person of the Son is an actual reality, as a matter of
fact a figure, that is, an image. Dogmatically, there is
no schism between image and word. In Jesus Christ,
the Word coincides with Him, with His Person. The
Person of Christ is concrete and real, because Christ
lives in wholeness and in the historical dimension.

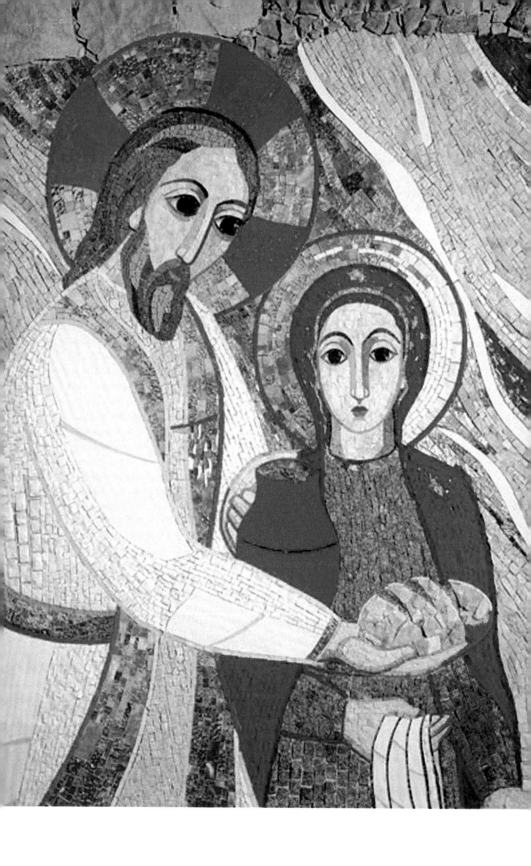

Image constitutes an integral part of liturgical space, of liturgy. Liturgy is an event, the most complete reality there is. It is an encounter, a celebration of God's love and of man's redemption.

Liturgy is an event of the Church. The Church cannot be reduced to specific sociological categories, but is divine-human, historical, and trans-historical in reality. It is a community that unites the living people of today with those who are already completely with God, in the Heavenly Church. We who are moving through history find in the liturgy a convocation, a true synaxis (assembly) with previous generations who are consecrated in Christ through the Holy Spirit. The faces and the gestures of those persons, together with the Theotokos, Jesus Christ, and the patriarchs and prophets of the Old Testament, live with us on the Church's path. Therefore, it seems particularly important to me to vivify today's church space with art, because it is vitally important that a modern man experience the Church community when he crosses a church's threshold. He should find in a church – even when it is empty –, faces, persons, and a whole world inhabited by the saved. This art should be capable not only of depicting but of manifesting the tangible presence of love and friendship in the church, so that he himself feels a part of it when he walks in.

*Marko Rupnik*
**Christ with Mother of God offers Bread and Wine,**
Chapel in Kochevski Rog, Kochevje – Slovenia, May 2005

**Fr. Stamatis:** The role of art is very important in the life of Church. We could say that the role of ecclesiastical art is to establish the clear and living presence of Christ and the Saints within the Holy Eucharist. Here, we should make note of the following: we are not talking about simply an

aesthetic and decorative role. In the theology of the
Fathers of the Church, ecclesiastical art took on
ontological meaning. This means, **first,** that we do
not paint the walls of the church simply to adorn
them; instead, this painting has an actual goal – to
reveal that in the moment when the faithful are
gathering together, assembling for the service of the
Holy Eucharist, Christ, the Most Holy Theotokos, the
Angels, and all the Saints are present with them.
**Second,** this means that the Church, when serving
the Holy Eucharist, iconizes the Kingdom of Heaven,
meaning Paradise, that is, a garden. It iconizes Eden
with the image of a garden. That is why all around
the saints there are decorative motifs that are taken
from the plant kingdom, from plants, from flowers.
There are petals, buds, leaves, and blooms, although
they are painted in a way only schematically and
geometrically. **Third,** this painting does not remind
us of something that happened in the past, but rather
of the event that is going on in the past; the Passion
of Christ, for example, or the martyrdoms of the
saints, and is transferred to the future, to a different
space and time, different from this unredeemed
space-time in which we live now in history. So it is
all about depicting the future, and not about
depicting the past. That kind of painting transforms
our life and represents it the way it is going to be in
Heaven – that is, freed from the fear of dying and
loosed from the bonds of corruptibility. **Fourth,**
considering that all other forms of painting are
within the boundaries of the corruptible mode of
human existence, it follows that ecclesiastical
painting has in it a certain ontological originality. It
refers to something completely new, just like Christ

is the only new thing under the sun, as St. John Damascene said. In the same way, an icon represents everything, man and nature, in a completely new, original, and authentic manner. **Fifth,** to indicate the new and original in a painterly way, the icon painter takes his inspiration from the Resurrection of Christ, Christ's appearances after the Resurrection, and the miracles that happened in the lives of saints. **Sixth,** in accordance with this, ecclesiastical painting is the painting of a vision that should therefore be, so to say, peculiar and surreal, because otherwise, it would not render the world to come, but the world of corruptibility, the world within history. And finally, **seventh,** since this is the case, it follows that an icon painter is a painter who, while painting, is constantly innovating, having freedom in painting methods and manners. In this way, the uniqueness and the distinctiveness of Byzantine painting in relation to other painting traditions is explained. Sadly, in our time, or, more precisely, in the last two centuries, Orthodox ecclesiastical painting has not been characterized by this authenticity and originality. Church painters adopt readymade solutions from the past and they do not paint Christ and His Kingdom with the painterly freedom that the Byzantine painters had.

### 2. Is contemporary ecclesiastical art in crisis in West and East?

**Fr. Stamatis:** Certainly. The crisis is, we could say, ontological, not just aesthetic and stylistic. The problem in contemporary ecclesiastical art is not primarily painterly, but theological. Keeping with

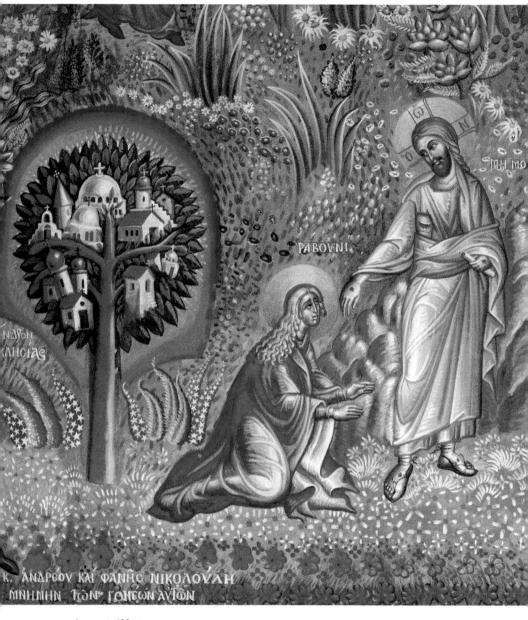

*Stamatis Skliris*
**Appearance of the Lord to Mary Magdalene,**
acrylic on wall,
St Nectarius Church, Voula – Greece, 2009

what we said in response to the first question, the icon painter is called to represent the Eschaton in a painterly way. That gives him an ontological freedom. I believe that often the modern icon painter errs; while he is in search of originality, he is looking for an aesthetical freedom rather than an ontological one. What do I mean by this? A painter may be talented, and it may be that he wants to find some new colors or new contours, something, some detail that did not exist in the painting of Studenica or Sopochani, but that he does not feel the need to present, in a painterly way, Christ as a completely new Man, that is, like a Man no one has ever seen before. We should keep in mind that icon painting is an art of vision, hence an art that depicts visions, and not the mundane everyday life and routine; the vision is what brings freedom into the painting of icons and it stems from how authentically the icon painter experiences the Holy Mystery of the Eucharist and the Church in general. Hence, the crisis of contemporary icon painting is, above all, a crisis of a theological nature. And to define that even more precisely, it is a crisis of the way in which we perceive freedom. Today's understanding of freedom is "how can I be free from something?" while the ontological understanding is "how can I free myself from corruptibility and from the mentality of corruptibility and from the passions that keep me tied to corruptibility, and to live the only new thing under the Sun, i.e. to live in a Resurrectional way that overcomes the misery of death and corruptibility?" Everything we have said in this response refers to the ecclesiastical art of the Orthodox East (and by East we mean a spiritual and

11

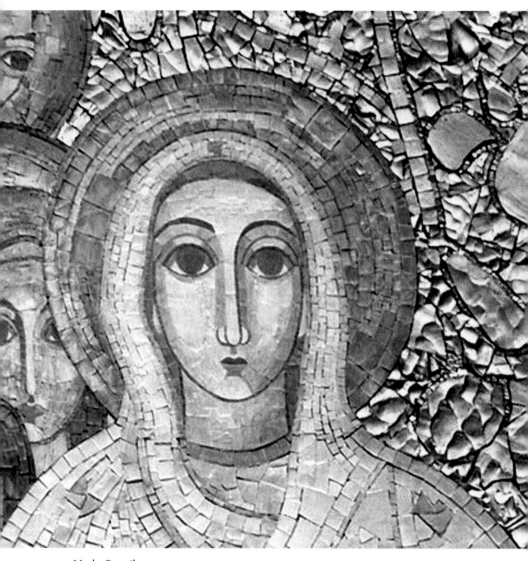

*Marko Rupnik*
**Detail,**
New Sanctuary of Saint Trinity,
Fatima – Portugal, September 2007

not geographical space). The crisis is even more significant in Orthodoxy, because Orthodoxy, through its manner of icon painting, iconizes, presents, and announces the Eschaton, the Kingdom of God, the Resurrection, and overcoming of corruptibility. For Western painting, the problem is not so significant, because as it is, in Western painting, light, which plays the main role in painting, is a natural and aesthetic light. Thus Western painting can experience a renewal from a purely aesthetic perspective, because, by the nature of things, it does not approach the icon ontologically.

**Fr. Marko:** I think the last centuries have experienced a crisis in ecclesiastical art in both East and West. The first millennium was marked by the Eastern Church's enculturation in various dynamic national and cultural contexts – just think of chanting, first Byzantine and later Byzantine-Slavic, too. The Catholic Church, on the other hand, remained static.

The end of the second millennium witnessed drastic changes. The Catholic Church underwent a strong process of enculturation in a historical and economic sense, as opposed to the Eastern Church, which slowly came to a halt. This has brought about a great change in the arts. The Catholic Church started opening up to new cultural and artistic horizons, but, unfortunately, with a less critical approach. The strong influence of Protestantism caused ecclesiastical art to become more absent, favoring empty space. This was in line with modern architecture's preference for an analysis of space within itself and for itself, with mathematic and

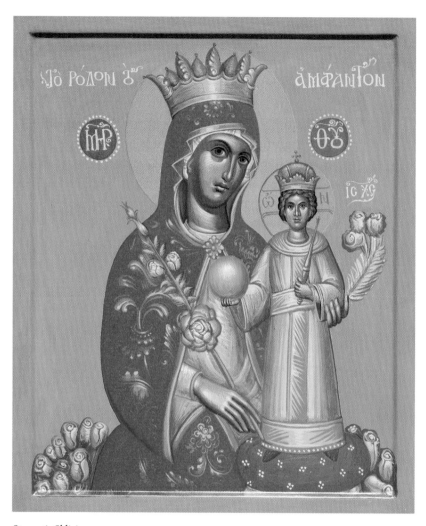

*Stamatis Skliris*
**Panagia, "Rodon to Amaranton"**
**(The Unwithered Rose),**
egg tempera on wooden board, 2007

geometric categories far removed from an organic approach.

Contemporary and modern art, with its absolute affirmation of the individual, revealed a positive aspect too, because in a culture that is impersonal above all, in which object dominates the whole anthropological horizon, art becomes a space for protest, striving to acknowledge everything that has been violated, perhaps unnoticed, in man or even crushed altogether.

Naturally, an art so strongly marked in its expression and language by intense subjectivism cannot find a place in the language of liturgy. As we know, liturgy has a purified language of companionship, in which communication has priority. The focus is on personal experience, which becomes woven into the organism of community. In liturgy, the organic relationship between person and community, between subjective and objective, is intertwined. Examining ecclesiastical art in the last ten years, we must say that the Catholic Church has evinced great courage on the one hand, and great confusion on the other. A division between art and liturgy has emerged. We have the moving testimony of Pope Paul VI, who begged artists for forgiveness for the schism that arose between the Church and art, a schism that damages both sides. Pope Paul VI said: "Art without the presence of the mystery of faith becomes void and a mere formalistic game, and the Church without art becomes crippled and dull."

In the East, the problem manifested itself differently. After a great flourishing of icon painting, fresco painting and mosaics, the process of enculturation – perhaps the most successful one in Christian history,

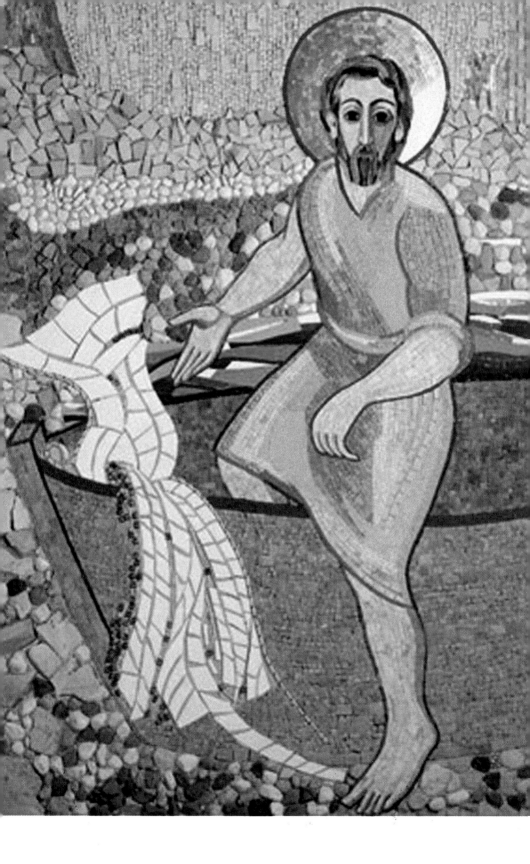

in which the presence of tradition was a vibrant stimulus to the arts – ended. The living wisdom of the Church incorporated icon painting in each new time period like a living organism and the icon painter, through memory, led himself to express his content. That is why great icon painters were neither imitators nor copyists, but they were obedient to the tradition of memory, and they were guided by the wisdom of the Church. The religiousness and sacredness of their art lay in the knowledge and keeping of tradition, the canons, and the Church in its entirety. Because of that their icon painting was living.

After the 14th and 15th centuries, a certain "sclerosis" appeared, a disease that wanted to hold back and restrain the process of development; this began a new period in which it was easy to stray into formalism, which led to copying and imitating the works of the great period.

A disparity developed that needs to be noted: the link between faith, spirituality, and Church life – to which the works of the previous period testified – was missing. An imitation of the worst kind of ecclesiastical art of the Western churches can be found in some famous monasteries and Orthodox churches.

*Marko Rupnik*
**St Peter Leaves the Boat and Nets and follows Christ's call,**
Chapel of Apostolic Nunciature,
Paris – France,
October 2003 -
- August 2004

Regarding the process of the revival of Byzantine iconography in the 20th century, I hear many Orthodox believers complaining about too many imitations and copies, because they threaten to subject everything to mere cosmetics. An Orthodox was explaining to me that, in his view, copies are always anemic, which is a betrayal of ecclesiality, because the copyist is paying so much attention to

17

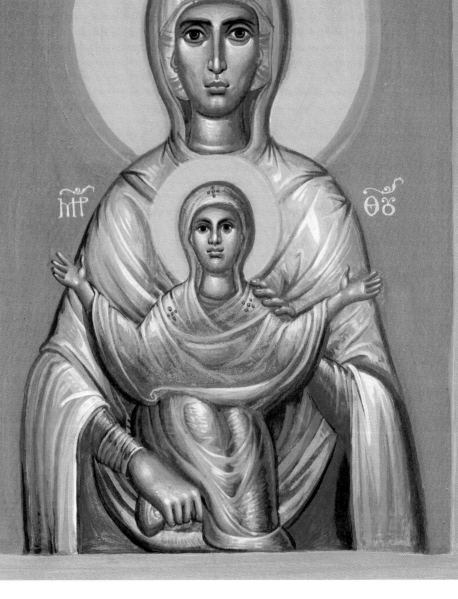

the form of what he needs to reproduce that he loses focus on the message he needs to convey through the icon. Thus, he forgets about the one to whom he needs to convey this message. Two important parts of iconography are life and communication in the Church, and these cannot be separated from the content of the faith. Christian art influenced history primarily through the communication that it provided. Art is a meeting place that reveals the spiritual, celestial, ecclesial, and fraternal dimensions. I believe that today serious attempts are being made in both East and West to overcome this crisis. In the West, these efforts are directed toward the restoration of the objective (hence, the traditional) aspect of ecclesiastical memory; every effort is being made to find a way to integrate into the contemporary culture in which we live. In the East, I continually see attempts at revival, through modern pursuits, in the arts, the sensibility of the Church itself, and the great icon painting canons. Here, I am referring mainly to obedience to the canons, but also to giving new life to language, by searching for a way for the canons to speak to us today and to be integrally respected. Orthodox people with whom I have spoken feel a strong need to create a bridge with a modern man, without the loss of the identity and richness of Tradition. This is a challenge also for me as a Catholic.

*Stamatis Skliris*
**Saint Ana,**
egg tempera on
wooden board, 2007

*3. To what extent did Impressionism, Expressionism, Cubism, Surrealism and Abstract painting influence contemporary ecclesiastical painting (if they did at all)?*

19

**Fr. Marko:** In Russia, in the beginning of the 20<sup>th</sup> century, artistic experiments took place in which traditional Orthodox artists took into consideration the artistic advances of their day. Unfortunately, as we know very well, political relations between the regime, the Church, and highly-spirited groups of intellectuals were not just problematic, but also dramatic. Because of that, these attempts remained isolated and most of them were eliminated from the Church horizon. Perhaps this is one of the many reasons why the Russian Orthodox Church is in a state of isolation within present-day Russia. The inability to dialogue with modern man is a sign of the faith's weakness. Holy Scripture and the Fathers, such as the Cappadocians, teach us that the one, who does not believe falls into isolation, narcissistically falls in love with himself, and is afraid of what is different and provocative on the cultural horizon. Impressionism, Expressionism, Cubism, Surrealism and Abstract art are not things which can be understood one-sidedly. They are very complex phenomena. After thirty years of study, I have found in some of these artistic phenomena similarities and affiliations with profound Christian theology, which would surprise or even shock those who have secluded themselves out of fear. There are examples of Abstract art and Arte Povera that allow Christians to express the dogma of creation and redemption, which perhaps up till now could not have been expressed. Saint Maximus the Confessor's theology of creation can be expressed in a new mosaic language in ways the medieval mosaicists could not express it. Considering today's environmental awareness, this could prove quite popular. Obviously, the question cannot be how we can improve icon painting with the help of the avant-garde of the 20th century. That would have been, and in some cases is, an artificial intervention without any credibility. It becomes something sterile, like everything "neo" – for example, neo-Gothic in the West, and neo-Byzantine in the East. Rather, what we're talking about is the possibility that one may achieve, through spiritual study, a serious, just, and conscientious spiritual life and Church prayer, the sight and vision that the holy icon painters had. And then one can search to express it in art in the language of contemporary developments. The great Patriarch Athenagoras spoke of the urgent need to reach this conclusion, so that we would not face the risk of turning the message into something ossified and sterile. The risk in the West lies in the danger of subjectivism and psychologisms.

**Fr. Stamatis:** First of all, we should note that all these movements that belong to what we refer to as Modern art are things that developed much later than the ecclesiastical painting tradition. We could even say that the first modernism in world history was founded not in the 19th century by Western art movements, but in Byzantium. If the essence of modernism lies in the liberation from classical conceptions of painting and the deliberate change of the canons and introduction of new ones, then that happened for the first time in Byzantium, when a change occurred in relation to the Classical, Hellenistic, and Greco-Roman artistic tradition. In the West, Modernism appeared as a reaction to the Renaissance. When El Greco was changing forms

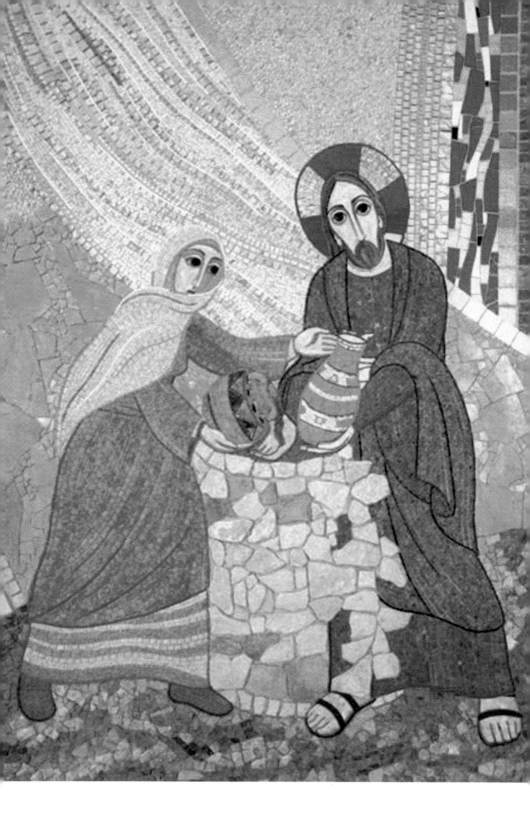

and colors and when his followers, Cezanne and later Picasso, continued toward an even more radical shift from the canons of classical Renaissance thought, they created western Modernism – a new way of perceiving things. However, art historians have failed to notice that something analogous happened many centuries before. When the first Christians started painting catacombs, they adopted the existing artistic ideas from Greco-Roman art, which were a continuation of Classical Greek art. Very soon however, inspired by the Resurrection and the victory over death, Christians discovered a new kind of painting with new stylistic and methodological tenets and principles that present a new understanding of the way we perceive the world. Traditional analogy, symmetry, and harmony gave way to facial expression and the expression of eyes (the gaze). In traditional sculpture particularly, the eyes were treated as one of the anatomic elements of the face and therefore had to be incorporated using the existing rules of analogy. In Byzantine painting, on the other hand, the expression of the eyes is considered so important that the aforementioned rules are transcended, and the eyes are painted bigger and more expressive in icons. Byzantine painting hence does not follow the laws of analogy, but focuses on facial expression and the liberation of depiction from the rules of perspective and color, and from the rules of natural shading. This bold and daring step that Christians took in ecclesiastical art was a modernism before Modernism. Orthodoxy's ecclesiastical art thus essentially brought a kind of Impressionism, Expressionism, Cubism, Surrealism, and Abstract Art into the classic art of that time.

*Marko Rupnik*
**Jesus and**
**Samaritan Woman,**
Church of Our Lady,
Jall Eddib – Lebanon,
June 2008

23

Therefore, it does not have any reason to envy
Western Modernism, since it already had it. For
example, we could say that the decorative leaves in
the mosaics in Ravenna, which color shades with
blue, accomplish, contrary to Classical Antiquity,
something similar and corresponding to the colors
of Van Gogh, which depict shadows as illuminated
and colored, more precisely, often as blue and purple.
Another example: when Christian icon painters,
instead of reducing depth of field, actually open it up
and create reverse perspective, they are doing
something similar to Picasso, Delauney, Braque,
expressionists, and cubists. When, in a Byzantine
fresco, the Samaritan woman at the well carries a
vessel that is bigger than the mouth of the well itself,
that, in fact, represents a surreal pictorial. We are
talking about something that cannot take place in
the natural world, but happens only under
supernatural circumstances. In brief, all the
peculiarities of Byzantine painting, which is inspired
by the Resurrection and overcoming of corruptibility,
contain within them a sense of challenge to the
natural state of things, and, therefore, represent the
first modernism in the history of world art. In spite
of the fact that, as we mentioned, ecclesiastical
painting contained within itself a certain kind of
modernism before the appearance of Western
Modernism, the dynamic relationship that develops
between civilizations, particularly between East and
West in our time, causes an icon painter to re-
examine the issue of shading and the treatment of
color and to be inspired, to some extent, by the
achievements of Western Modernism.
As for the possible influence of Modernism on

Orthodox icon painting, I personally cannot conceive a living Christian painter of the 21st century who would live in such a way as to ignore and disregard the great achievements of Western art history, like Impressionism for example, and who would be able to live isolated from the problems that surround modern man. On account of this, I assume that every Christian, or at least one who is moved by love, cares and shows interest in the problems that preoccupy his fellow man, regardless of where he lives, in the West or in the East. Unfortunately, this way of thinking does not concern modern icon painting as much as one might expect.

*4. Is there such a thing as original Christian icon painting today or does replicating dominate?*

**Fr. Stamatis:** Authenticity is foremost a spiritual problem, and only secondarily a painterly problem. First, when authenticity in the way in which the Holy Eucharist, Christ, and love for fellow man are lived and experienced is lost, this is then reflected in ecclesiastic painting through the phenomenon of replication. We should accept and acknowledge the fact that there are, for example, many Christians who copy, in the spiritual life, the demeanor of their spiritual father outwardly, as if spiritual life is a matter of demeanor and not of inner experience. We would like to say something that concerns those who claim that Tradition is a continuous process of replication, in which new icon painters replicate old ones and in which everything new is considered to be less worthy than everything old. This concept is, foremost, radically Platonistic, hence Hellenistic and un-Christian. In Plato's system of ideas it is

25

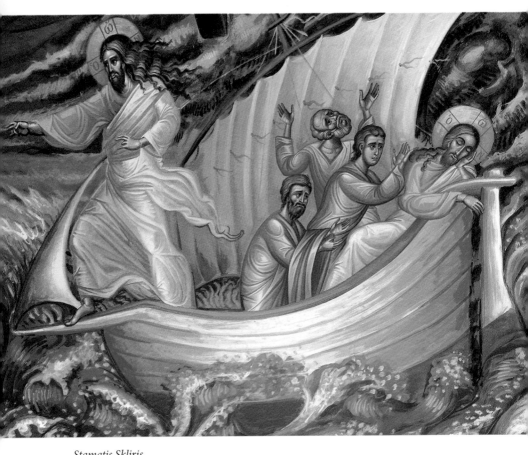

*Stamatis Skliris*
**Christ Calms The Sea,**
acrylic, St Panteleimon Church, Athens, 2009

understood that ideas present perfect prototypes and that any subsequent realization of an idea is deemed less valuable than the prototype. We have a big problem if the same holds true for Christianity. According to St. Maximus the Confessor, truth will be manifested in the Eschaton, while now we are living in an icon of the truth — that is, something less than perfect. This reversal of matters in relation to Platonism gives the icon the freedom we talked about and opens our horizons, our minds, and our lives to another kind of existence that is completely new. Herein lies the authenticity of Orthodox icon painting and thus there are no reasons for replicating in the strict sense of the word.

**Fr. Marko:** If "original" stands for the synthesis between the objectivity of the divine revelation and our acceptance of it, then original is a dynamic relationship between Christ, Who is revealed and celebrated in the Church's liturgy, and our reception of Him, our perception and proclamation of salvation. In that case, we could say that Christ, true God and true Man, Lord and our Savior, is colored by our colors too, because we are woven into Him through our baptism and He passes into the world through us who constitute His Church. Those are the things that are unchangeable. Dogmas are unchangeable, but the ways of comprehending and interpreting them are marked by different cultures and times. But it is exactly this dynamic relationship that is a necessary characteristic of the Church. Confusion between dogmas and dogmatism is suicide for the faith. I think that in the last ten years, in the Catholic Church and in some Orthodox Churches, traces of some achievements of that kind

of art can be observed, of art which is a result of a
synthesis of that which was received and that which
is conveyed. Originality that is understood as a
pursuit for the language of unique forms, primarily
subjective ones in which the subject is being self-
affirmed, eventually become eliminated by the
believers, that is, by the Church itself. Originality as
self-affirmation of an individual has no place in
ecclesiality, which is a harmonious relationship
between the individual and the community. In the
East, the problem of replication is more prevalent.
But this is somewhat of a surprise considering that
replication is a post-modern phenomenon. It is
strange that the tendency toward replication and
imitation is most strongly marked today in the
former communist bloc. But as the great scholars of
cultural anthropology say, the phenomenon of Post-
Modernism is still insufficiently analyzed and
deciphered, and that is true for both East and West.
The Post-Modernistic climate is one of frailty of
identity, and intellectual and spiritual insecurity.
Because of that, there is a strong need for
identification, for attaching oneself to modules that
have already been used, for representation through
prefabricated, artificially adopted languages. After
totalitarian and atheistic regimes, in the face of
terrifying and unsettling liberalism, this could turn
out to be an excellent trap. In fact, I have found
various spaces created by copyists that have a mystic
setting with candles and prayers, but lack any
opportunity for communication and contact with
people. Keeping in mind what St. John the Apostle
says in his first letter, we are confused because mercy
and love are integral parts of faith. One cannot

proclaim Christ on the one hand, and not be able to love one's neighbor on the other. This is another trap. The great tradition of Christian art in both East and West was born within Church life and not from false motives.

## 5. What is the main distinction between secular painting and icon painting?

**Fr. Marko:** We could say that art inspires adoration, and ecclesiastical art dedication and reverence. In a certain sense, the art of the last century did not want to inspire adoration. The art of the 20th century did not want to be beautiful. The concept of beauty, once discarded by theology, and then taken up by philosophical idealism and Romanticism, was completely rejected by the art of 20th century. This is an art of intense, firm, and direct artistic expression – the confession of a modern man. The gallery has become a confessional. It has to be approached with great reverence, piety, and mercy. The art of the 20th century is the heart of modern man turned inside-out. This art bears the presence of pain and darkness. Ecclesiastical art, on the other hand, draws man into its dramatic subject and presents him in the light; it carries him into the contemplation of salvation. Therefore it is possible to create it from the experience of salvation, experienced by the saved mankind that is the Church. Ecclesiastical art is not spiteful; it does not look down on other arts. It is the art of compassion and the testimony of God's mercy. On account of that, its language cannot be subjected to aesthetic and artistic criteria, without liturgy and theology. Theological and liturgical criteria cannot

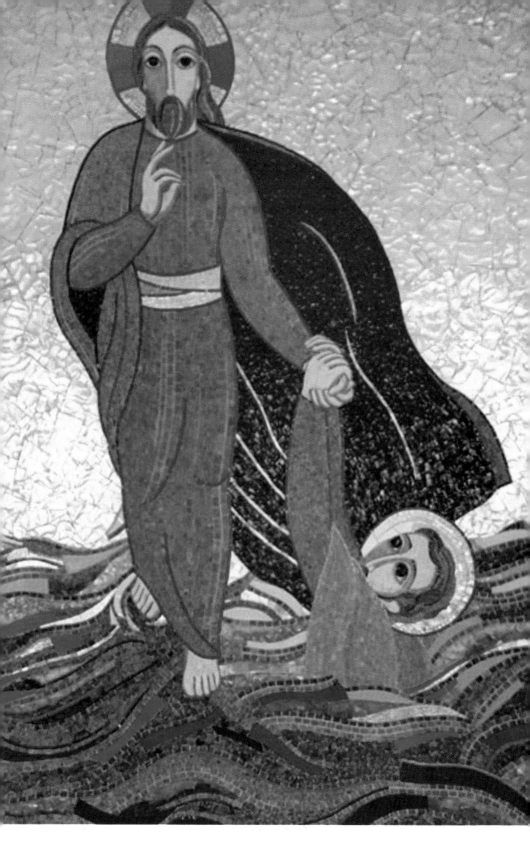

be determined solely by the past, because the Church is a treasury of faith and the key to the door to the wealth and gifts of the Holy Spirit. Hence, the relationship between good artists and Church has to be stern, spiritual, and on a high intellectual and cultural level. I personally experienced that grace during the great pontificate of John Paul II.

**Fr. Stamatis:** The most common reply is that ecclesiastical painting and icon painting obey the canons of ecclesiastical tradition, while secular painting is free to depict things however it wants. As we said before, an icon's freedom is an ontological freedom, that is, freedom from the laws of nature, which are the laws that lead to corruptibility. Thus, according to this, a reply like the previous one is not complete because it does not make a distinction between different understandings of the concept of freedom. We could distinguish these two arts the following way: icon painting is a painting that iconizes beings the way they are going to be in the future, while secular paintings depicts them the way they were in the past. Even though this definition is very brief, it is still quite comprehensive, because it describes in few words the main features of two pictorial concepts. Secular painting is confined to the limits of time, thus, to the laws of time and place, and accordingly, to corruptibility, inasmuch as it paints something already belongs to the past. Conversely, the icon is headed toward the Resurrection of all of nature and it iconizes beings in the way they are going to be after the Resurrection, in the eternal life; accordingly, it represents an art of the future. We owe a definition like this one, based

*Marko Rupnik*
**Christ and St Peter Walking on the Sea,** Chapel of Sister the Sole on River, Rijeka – Croatia, October 2008

on a distinction between past and future, to a great theologian, the metropolitan bishop of Pergamon, John Zizioulas. Without his teaching on ontology, we might have not been able to formulate such a concise and effective definition. Even though this definition seems theological, philosophical, and theoretical, and therefore as if it has nothing to do with the method of painting, it does contain all of the characteristic qualities that distinguish one art from the other. Icon painting, as an art of future, depicts time and place saved from corruptibility. On account of that, shadings cannot be painted, because they remind us of death. Design in an icon should not delineate remoteness, distance between beings; therefore, it cannot have the usual geometric perspective that distances and minimizes beings. Thus beings cannot be painted in a way as to give off an impression of weight, thickness and overall features; they cannot be painted in a way that would indicate they are dominated, inevitably, by the laws of nature.

If we are to make this kind of distinction between secular and ecclesiastical art, then we should admit there are works of art that are painted as secular, but incline toward the icon and are in fact very close to an icon. A still life by Van Gogh, in which the depicted garlic shines with a light that seems incorruptible, functions within the logic system of the icon. Some Orthodox Christians want to emphasize that iconography is not painting, and consequently claim that there is painting, which we refer to as secular painting, and then there is the icon, which is not painting. We have to respond to this. I would say that iconography most certainly is painting. It consists of shapes, colors, and to some extent, it has volume and plasticity, because between the basic color of the body, which designates darkened parts, and the light, which designates facial and body parts that are more prominent, there is a certain space that is formed and defined.

Accordingly, iconography is painting. It is painting that shows beings that exist in a different mode of existence, different from the mode of corruptibility. It is a painting which we might call "Paschal," even though the word Paschal does not refer to pictorial qualities. It is a theological expression. We might, however, say that the pictorial qualities are so influenced by faith in the Resurrection that they represent a transfigured world in an icon. If icon in fact is a painting of resurrection, a painting that saves beings from corruptibility and represents them as if they were monumental (μνημειακά: the real meaning of the term refers not to size and grandeur, but to the fact that a being remains remembered forever and is never forgotten), then we can claim that the most significant form of painting is indeed iconography. We are rephrasing the previous dilemma – the claim of some that iconography is not painting – and saying not only that it is painting, but that it is, in fact, the most significant painting. It is actually the fulfillment of the purpose of painting in an absolute sense, because, since the earliest times of cave painting, painting has, by depicting a being, rescued it from oblivion, giving him a sort of immortality, because a work of art cannot be lost and forgotten. If this is one of the main purposes of art, then iconography is an art above all others, painting par excellence. With an approach to matters like this

33

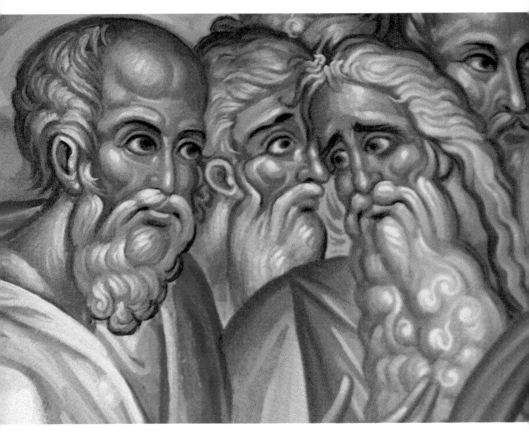

*Stamatis Skliris*
**Resurrection, detail,**
acrylic on wall,
St Nectarius Church, Voula – Greece, 2009

one, we are preserving iconography as painting, and we are also preserving iconography's relationship with secular painting, because we are viewing it as something that exists in a dialectic relation. Perhaps iconography is something other than painting, but it is also painting. It is exactly what the Church is to the world: the Church is in this world, it is the world, but it is also something different from the world, a foretaste of the Kingdom of God, and by being something else, something different, it saves the world. Instead of claiming that iconography has no relationship to painting, it is better to say that it is a form of painting that saves painting, because it succeeds in achieving the great aims of painting throughout time.

*6. What is an icon to you? What is the difference between iconography and religious painting and painting in general?*

**Fr. Stamatis**: I pointed out in the previous response that iconography is a painting that depicts human beings in the way they are going to be, in a different mode of existence, in the Eschaton, that is, in the Kingdom of Heaven. I could give a different definition that the icon is a portrait of Christ, but a special kind of portrait that shows Him as an entirely new Man, a Man that has never been seen before. This kind of definition implies that Christ is the God-Man and consequently that He has a kind of charisma that is impossible to find in any other man. That is the reality we refer to as "something other," something which is beyond nature. It is human and divine, combined in one hypostasis — in the divinity of Christ, which both Western and Eastern Church

35

believe. But technically, stylistically, it is expressed only in the Eastern icon, not in Western painting, which is always more focused on the human nature of Christ. Thus, religious painting shows the personality of Christ with a portrait of the historical Christ. It demonstrates Christ as a man, the way men of His time saw Him, without showing on His face and expression that He is true God and true Man. We could say that it paints the world the way it is in the world of corruptibility and unsaved time and place. Religious painting depicts Christ and the saints who lead the world toward overcoming corruptibility, but it paints them in a pictorial manner as the historical Christ and the historical saints, the way they were when they lived here on earth — thus with all the characteristics of human nature. The icon, on the other hand, possesses that crucial difference in that it does not depict the historical Christ, but rather the eschatological Christ and the saints as they are going to be in their eschatological state. Thus, painting and religious painting depict the past, and iconography reveals the future.

**Fr. Marko:** To me, an icon is, above all, a spiritual presence. However, an icon is so effective in its message because it has a simple language that gives image to the mystery. It is obvious that in this sense the icon is inexpendable. Early Christian art, the art of the first centuries of Christianity, is completely imbued with the presence of God. Pre-Romanesque and Romanesque art are not any less important than icons. We should beware not to forget some of the great Christian periods. I'd like to tell you a story:

with deep affection I experienced something that is reminiscent of an icon's power. In an Orthodox church in Romania, I was working on the apse, and when I brought the image of the Theotokos to show it to the Metropolitan, while the mosaic was still attached to the wooden board and displayed in the church, a line of faithful formed, young and old, who came to kiss and pray in front of the image. It seems to me, that an icon can be considered, in dogmatic terms, canonical, if it comes from art which, along with the matter and language it uses, is also flooded with the love of God, which arouses reverence and induces pure religious countenance. A true theology of the creation of the material world is needed for this, a deep theological vision of work and human creativity, and above all, the testimony of the Church who prays before that painting. This is a synthesis of what St. John Damascene has left us.

### 7. How is iconography perceived in the Western Christian tradition, and how is it perceived in the Eastern?

**Fr. Marko:** After 1200 AD, the ecclesiastical art of the Catholic Church diverged from its roots, which stem from the Eastern Church. With the emigration of Russians after the Bolshevik Revolution, the West discovered the icon. Mostly owing to faithful Russians, and theologians such as Evdokimov, Florensky, and Ouspensky, the West became familiar with the icon. I find that to be an important symptom of something deeper. In a civilization with a proliferation of images, a need arises for two things. Before a subjective language comes a need for a language of community, thus, for communication. In

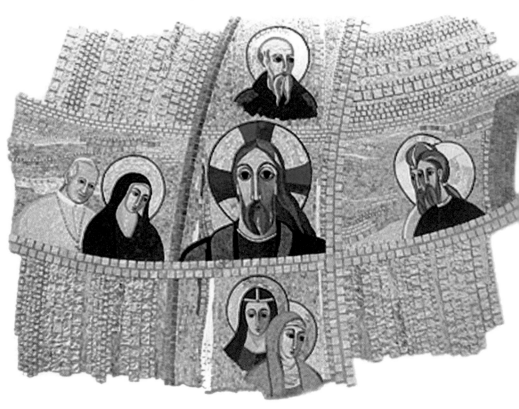

*Marko Rupnik*
**Look at the whole,**
Capitel Hall in the Residence of the Catholic Archbishop,
Ordinariat of Archbishop,
Belgrade – Serbia, September 2006

that matter, the icon is helpful. On the other hand, before a tide of bodily and sensual images, there emerges a need for a spiritual image. That is, for an image that directs you toward a better way of living, a higher level of thinking, and opens up the world on high. And to this as well, the icon comes as a great aid. We should also note that along with the icon, the West grasped the appeal, importance, and verity of artistic eras that were overtly spiritual, such as the Early Christian, Early Romanesque, Romanesque, etc.

Today, one can see that the West is losing interest in the icon. The icon seems too strange and removed from the cultural and ecclesiastical milieu. It appears as something exotic, and thus, passes out of fashion. Because of some imitators with ideological and fanatical attitudes, drastic reactions can be noted, like the dismissal of things that are too artificial and cosmetic. On the other hand, the attempts of those who were inspired by icons created a new reality, which is appreciated, as Cardinal Spidlik says.

**Fr. Stamatis:** In the West, religious painting points our attention to the past, reminding us of the works of Christ and His words, and inspires our feelings of devoutness. It carries an ethical message as well. Because of that, it is a useful painting in a religious sense.

In the East, an icon, inasmuch as it reveals the Eschaton, possesses a dimension that is purely liturgical, and not psychological or ethical. Thus, the eschatological Christ does not make us a little bit better as people, but leads us to the conclusion of history when what remains will be judged, as well as what has an eternal value from all that we have created in terms of our deeds in the time of our earthly life. In the East, the icon is included in an iconological vocabulary that is used by Church, in a more general sense. The entire Holy Liturgy is a language that speaks through icons; it is a great icon of the Eschaton. The bishop, surrounded by presbyters and deacons, leads us to the Kingdom of Heaven during the Holy Eucharist like an icon that is set before us. The Gospel does this too, because it is gold or silver, and because it looks like a book that is different from all the other books we read. Besides that, every liturgical detail points toward the Kingdom of Heaven that is to come. Accordingly, the icon is not just a useful religious painting, but a manifestation and revelation of the reality that transcends our daily routine. It does not improve us somehow in an ethical sense, but reminds us that we are created for a completely different mode of existence than the one we are living in now.

*8. There is a notion that there is an increased interest in icon in the East and West.*
*How do you interpret that?*

**Fr. Stamatis:** Historically, emigrants that came from Russia to Europe after the Revolution made icons recognizable in the West. The development of historical studies too helped us perceive the icon with a new scientific interest. From the spiritual viewpoint, on the other hand, the interest in icons is mostly indebted to the fact that everyday life became so mundane and evil has multiplied to such an extent that we are now living in an apocalyptic era, that deep down, existentially, yearns for a revelation, a manifestation of a mode of existence that overcomes corruptibility. We could say that the more sin is multiplied, the more the longing within man increases, the longing for a thorough, ontological change. Lust for life, which is a lust for pleasure, contains in itself the lust for death. Then appear fear and an unquenchable desire for the Resurrection. At that moment the Orthodox icon encounters modern man.

**Fr. Marko:** The father of Russian Symbolism, Vyacheslav Ivanovich Ivanov, gave a good answer to this question. He supported the theory that, at one time, poets were priests and priests were poets, artists. Poets and priests are akin to midwives, who help babies be brought into the light of day; so poets and priests bring the real life into the light. In the Liturgy, and above all in the sacraments, the priest reveals the meaning of creation from the created itself. Water in the baptism becomes real water and sacramental bread becomes real bread. In the same way, the artist communicates with the meanings he derives from the real world and history. All reality is symbolic. It is symbolic in its authentic theological meaning: the presence of the Creator and Savior is reflected in everything. It is not about just attributing meaning (which is typical for subjective and intellectual art), but it is about revealing the signified. An artist must be ascetically pure because God reveals Himself to the pure and resists the proud. Reality is open, and in touch with men, the obedient ones, that is, the contemplative ones. As the fundamental agent in theology is the Holy Spirit, so in art, inspiration, as Soloviev says, is not from the muses, but from the Holy Spirit.

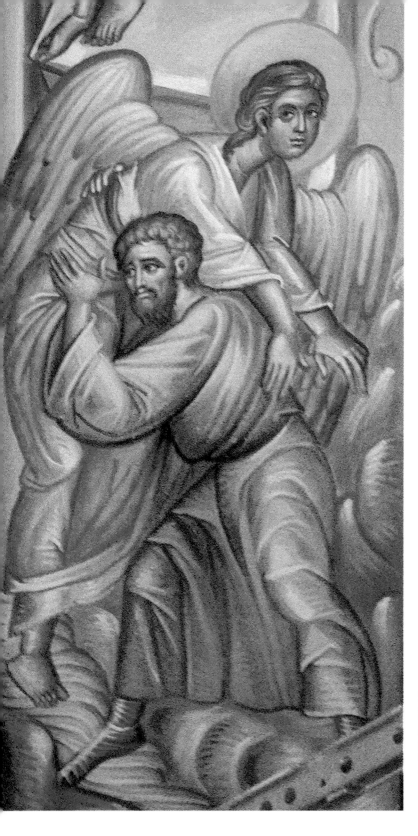

*Stamatis Skliris*
**Jacob Wrestles
with God,**
acrylic on wall,
St Nectarius
Church, Voula
– Greece, 2009

There is, in fact, the danger of falling into decadence, in the priesthood as well as in the artistic vocation. A priest might become a bureaucrat in an office, and an artist might become a mannerist, technically well trained, a good imitator and his art academically acclaimed. People have an authenticity sensor for identifying both. The people can come to understand a priest and trust him; similarly, in art, one can tell which painting is genuine, and which is a cosmetic product, which artist is spiritual and which one is not. The quality of their work is not equally appreciated by fellow artists and art critics. Many of the icons and paintings of the great sanctuaries of the West are very honored and venerated, but to authoritative art criticism they have no value.

*9. For a long time icon painters have been compared to priests. Why is that?*

**Fr. Stamatis**: I would say that the icon painter is more like an evangelist and a preacher of the Church than a priest. He preaches the Resurrection of Christ and the Kingdom of Heaven with colors. He preaches also that the holy men of God are those who have reached a level where already in this life they experienced a foretaste of the Kingdom of Heaven. A priest does something else. He brings the Kingdom of Heaven here and now by serving the Holy Eucharist.

*10. How can the freedom of artistic creativity be reconciled with the requirement to obey the iconographic canons? Is obedience to the canons a threat to the vitality of iconography?*

**Fr. Marko:** Before the Renaissance in the West the practice of an artist signing his works was practically unknown. The artist was in the service of the One who had something to say, who had a meaning to convey. In fact, the One was searching for someone who could represent Him. With the Renaissance began the modern age and the affirmation of the subject. Suddenly, the content and the presence of mystery have to be attributed to the importance of the artist. As part of that affirmation and one-sidedness of the subject, art became simply an expression of the artist and was confined to his perspective rather than that of the One to whom the artist was in service. Art, therefore, needs to overcome this kind of limitation and assert its freedom to be expressed in various ways. This goes in hand with the development of an atheistic culture that has no place for God, a culture in which man is self-sufficient. In a sense, Italy represents a case of particular significance. The Renaissance was born in Italy; it was a step in an important spiritual and intellectual development. The divine-human balance, which in the late Middle Ages reached a divine extreme and thus violated in some sense the dogma of the Council of Chalcedon, was counterweighted with a humanistic response. What is typically human is also spiritual, that is why God revealed Himself as a man. So Italy remains, in fact, the only European country (excluding the space within the Vatican borders) in which there was no anti-clerical and anti-Christian uprising. Protestant Germany and Orthodox Russia are two examples of bloody extremism. One of the greatest Russian intellectuals of our time, Sergei Averintsev, told me: "The tragedy of Russian Orthodox Christianity is that Russia is either one big monastery or one big army base." There is a great deal of truth in this statement. It shows how difficult it is to obtain a spiritual balance. The balance between the divine and the human is sociologically translated into the balance between freedom and obligation. This dichotomy is the Golgotha of European Christianity. This is not about prejudice between East and West. This is Golgotha. Looking at it, Serbia is taking its first steps in trying to say something too. In this climate of confusion and fog that covers the East and West of Europe, it is important for the artist to discover the meaning of external memory and history. Memory and history are the synthesis of objective and subjective. They help us learn to care about others, and when we learn that, the art of love – which is the service of others –should follow. Art loses its meaning if it is not useful to others. Art is service and the artist puts himself into that service. When the artist discovers that wisdom, he emerges from the tunnel and lives out his service as a joy and a delight of communicating with others. But here there is a contradiction, as in art: the more characteristic it is, the more it is universal. Most people today probably think that it is not so important to obey canons or their will, but rather the important thing is to learn how to love, to think with love, i.e., to think in consideration of others. Today, it has become a real challenge to capture the mind of the Church, in which obedience stands side-by-side with love. To learn how to live is to learn how to love, and the one who learns how to love learns also how to serve, live, and obey. And none of these three things is a

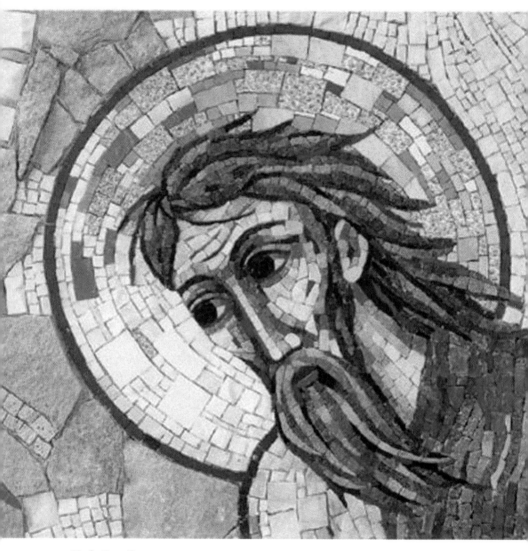

*Marko Rupnik*
**The Image of John the Baptist,**
Chapel at the Theological Seminary,
Maribor – Slovenia, September 2001

problem to him. Art that is made in this way is alive and enchanting. Art made solely out of obedience to canons is just dry and dull formalism. It is crucially important here to clarify what we mean by "canon." Cardinal Spidlik taught me that canon is conveyed personally, communally, and through the Church. It can be seen as something objective, and it is usually misinterpreted as a rule, as in some regime. To look at the canons is to look at the community of people in an ecclesiastical sense, the horizontal and vertical community, as they say.

**Fr. Stamatis:** If we look at the historical development of iconography, we will see that, up to the 17th century, it was constantly evolving. Hence, the canons do not restrain creativity. Even everyday life follows and obeys rules and, in fact, it is impossible to live if there is no obedience to rules. However, every creature of God lives for itself in an authentic way. Hence, the canons of life do not restrain authentic living. The question is then why, in the last centuries, we do not have real creativity? Instead, we see slavishness, as if we were slaves, so that copying prevails, dominating modern icon painting. It may be that we Orthodox Christians have not understood the true Orthodox canon of iconography, of icon painting. The rapid evolution of technology created a new understanding of copying. Now machines can make an absolute copy of something; before that, there was nothing that was absolutely identical to something else. Panselinos could not photograph the frescoes of some other icon painter and copy them. Also, he could not use a projector beam to project a design of some other painting in order to copy it exactly. We can set aside the essential problem that, in nature, there are no two identical things anyway. So let's raise the question of what is "canon" in Orthodox icon painting? Moreover, did the first hagiographers have an intention to set up some canons that the next hagiographers in the centuries to come would be obliged to follow with an absolute obedience? In Christ, the apostles, and the first Christians we find an authentic way of living in the community of love. That is the Church – a community of love that is identified with the Eschaton and the Holy Trinity, which is the community of love par excellence. In a similar way, the first icons possess the same spirit of yearning for the Kingdom of Heaven that is to come. The entire style and manner of Orthodox icon painting is inspired by the Resurrection, which brought about a completely new way of existence. Light plays the major role in this. We could even say that we could take an ancient Greek drawing, which represents a perfect drawing in any time period, and, by illuminating that ancient Greek and hence pre-Christian drawing, and composing the light in an iconographic manner, we could make it into an icon. If we understand what kind of transfiguration the divine grace, which is coming from the outside, brings into our life and into the world, then we can comprehend the secret of the canons in iconography. The canons and typikon of Orthodox icon painting are those constant features of painting that came from the inspiration that Christian painters received by living a different life, the foretaste of a different life. We can see that Byzantine painting is a painting with very strong, highlighted outlines, bold lines for

the eyes, nose, etc., and that is a stylized painting.
But it escapes our attention that the outline is thicker
the moment the light hits the relatively darker
primary color; that, in a way, represents a being,
represents a state before creation, hence the state
before God created beings out of nothing. This
dialectic between light and dark is what created the
"austerity" of Byzantine painting. It was not as if some
Christian painters said: "paint only with thick lines,"
but they participated and lived in that light and
experienced that other kind of light that enlightens
our dark existence. On the one hand, it gives us
eternal hypostasis, and on the other, it distinguishes
and evaluates things and then the difference between
light and dark is revealed.

Besides, modern art has shown that it is possible to
paint with dark outlines or with thick lines, as
Picasso did, and that artistic (painterly) strokes can
still be free and not stylistic.

### 11. What is the relation between contemporary theology and art?

**Fr. Stamatis:** First, we should say something about
the relationship between Orthodox and Western
theology. As we said before, Western theology is
historical and ethical, and Eastern is more mystical
and spiritual. For this mystical dimension, Russian
theologians are mostly responsible. With the
Western historical approach, when there is too much
historicism, there is a danger of coming to the point
of talking about matters that concern only the past
and not contemporary man. In the Russian approach,
there is a danger of falling into too much

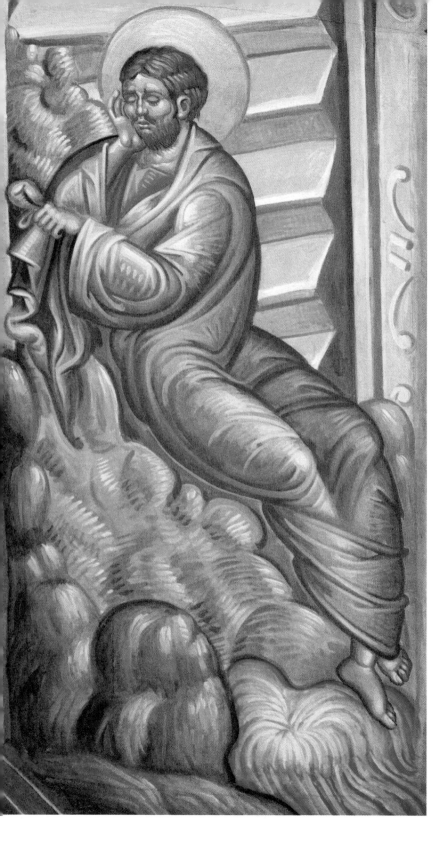

*Stamatis Skliris*
**Jakob's Dream,**
acrylic on wall,
St Nectarius
Church, Voula
– Greece, 2009

sentimentality and subjectivity. The Eucharist and its icon are safeguards against these dangers.

Contemporary icon painters, however, are confronted with both of these temptations – either to copy the past, or, fortunately less common, to introduce sentimental elements into the icon. Here I would like to express a personal impression. My view is that in Athens, a theology of ontology has developed in recent time, the great representative of which is Metropolitan John Zizioulas, along with Christos Yannaras and the theologian-philosopher Stelios Ramphos. Incidentally, at that very same, there appeared in Athens a small group of icon painters whose work manifests an authentic tendency* to express Orthodox liturgy in art. I believe that, when we are gone, they will talk about the theological school of Athens and the icon painting school of Athens, and that it occurred without any particular plan that would have consciously and intentionally created such a movement. Allow me to present another personal impression. Contemporary Serbian theologians are more aware of the crucial theological problems today than the theologians of other Orthodox nations are and today's Serbian icon painters are competent and well-equipped to deal with contemporary subjects in icon painting.

Unfortunately, our era is lacking something that is more crucial than anything else—holiness. If we did not believe in God's grace and God's providence, we would be in danger of falling into despair, considering how feebly we modern Christians,

---

* leaning

modern theologians, and modern icon painters live. Only holiness can attract the divine grace that is necessary for a genuinely authentic theology and authentic art. The other thing modern theologians lack (notable exceptions aside) is a genuinely and thoroughly philosophical way of thinking and facing matters, like the great theologians of the past, like the Cappadocians. Father Atanasije Jevtic told me many years ago that, as he studied the Cappadocian Fathers, he became convinced that their theological positions were inspired by the Holy Spirit, but were also aided by a great deal of education and study. We might add that the basic assumption was that they wanted to philosophize in a Greek way. On the other hand, contemporary icon painters do not work in a way that is fundamentally painterly. When you ask a question, you should know to philosophize, and the grace of God will help you find the answer. However, it is important what kind of question you ask. To ask painterly questions, you should, first of all, paint and then you will find painterly ways to express the truth of Orthodoxy.

**Fr. Marko:** The great Catholic theology of the 20th century, worked out by people like Danielou, Romano Guardini, Congar, and Balthazar, once again appreciated art in a useful way. Romano Guardini, above all, came to realize what threat the rejection of beauty posed to theology. The problem is, while these men brought beauty back into theology, they also brought with it philosophical idealisms and romanticisms, and thus resulted another problem: modern art, to these theologians, had nothing to do with beauty. Beauty is, on the one hand, considered

theologically as the embodiment of what is truthful
and good, an embodiment that is transfigured in
relation to reality and history. On the other hand, the
art of the 20th century did not want to be the
embodiment of what is good and truthful. The good
and the truthful are woven in this art mostly in a
subjective way in displays of pain and drama, as
protests against the lack of truth and absence of good.
They have come to consider as truthful only that
which reflects the real condition of a soul. Thanks to
some suggestions by John Paul II and Benedict XVI,
there is now the possibility for significant change.
John Paul claimed that art is a path of cognition, and
thus the gnoseology's deliverance from the
possessiveness of philosophical argumentative logic
or scientific methodology. "Art is an experience of
universality. It cannot be just an object or something
in between. It is a primitive word, meaning it comes
first and it stands at the end of every other word. It is
a word to be counted on, an identification of
experience, the first and the last significance of life.
Knowledge that is translated into lines, images, and
sounds, symbols that the mind can recognize as
projections of the mystery of life, beyond the limits
which conception cannot overcome: hence, art is an
opening into the depths, heights, and inexplicability
of existence, roads that lead man freely into the
mystery, and transform anxiety into something that
has no words with which to be expressed. Art is
religious because it leads man to the awareness of
anxiety that is deep inside his being, which science,
with the objective formality of its rules, or
technology, which is programmed to avoid any risk
of error, can never manage to satisfy."

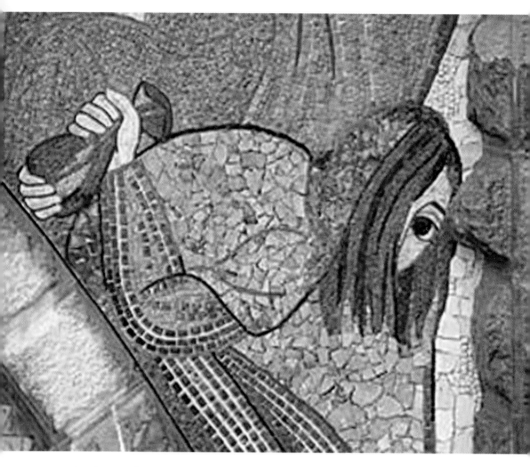

*Marko Rupnik*
**Judas Iskariot,**
Bazilica Rosemary Wreath,
Lourd – France, December 2007

(John Paul II addressing artists in the theater "La Fenice," in Venice on June 6, 1985.)

Benedict XVI, giving a short summary of the catechism of the Catholic Church, boldly states that art can express mysteries of faith better than words.

"These (artistic images) are drawn from the rich patrimony of Christian iconography. The centuries-old conciliar tradition teaches us that images are also preaching of the Gospel. Artists in every age have offered the principal facts of the mystery of salvation to the contemplation and wonder of believers by presenting them in the splendour of colour and in the perfection of beauty. It is an indication of how today more than ever, in a culture of images, a sacred image can express much more than what can be said in words, and be an extremely effective and dynamic way of communicating the Gospel message."

(Compendium of the Catechism of the Catholic Church. Introduction no. 5)

Personally, I am always studying Eastern theology, and I have a lot to learn from it, especially since in the East, art had a theological position, and since the Second Council of Nicaea, it is possible to be engaged in theology with words, images, and colors. I think that the Orthodox Church today could, with a little more boldness and determination, open up its treasures to a productive dialogue between theology and culture, especially art. Because the history of contemporary art shows us that, particularly in these countries, a great rift occurred between these two realities. Today, nobody can boast about having answers to these questions, but maybe God's mercy will spur us into an exchange of gifts in a way that we can together again become a driving force in culture, and art can become a place of spirituality.

## 12. Is the icon the best and most authentic painterly expression of the Christian faith?

**Fr. Marko:** I think it could be said with certainty that the icon is one of the most successful examples of the enculturation of the Christian faith. Having said that, I see only one problem. For various reasons, a stage was reached where icon painting no longer had any vitality, as if it had become sealed. There are, as I said, many reasons why the art of icons no longer had such a dynamic continuity of high quality. When reality stops pulsating, it is not a good sign. I cannot tell why an Eastern Church fresco from the late Middle Ages and some of the mosaics in the south of Italy are not equally authentic Christian expressions. I also cannot tell why the manger of St. Francis of Assisi could not be authentic. I would not dare say that the theology and spirituality of the Franciscan manger have a less intense quality than a Byzantine icon. It is about different approaches, different emphases, in no way antagonistic or contradictory, but complementary.

I believe that the art that has liturgy and theology as its material and aesthetic is the authentic exponent of Christian art. When we say theology and liturgy, we should understand them as the Holy Fathers did, as that which builds the foundation of the spiritual life, that is, life in the Holy Spirit. The Holy Spirit is life-giving, and theology is a sentient Church organism that has a thorough dynamic and it cannot be bound to only one place or one period of time. It would be contradictory to the core of our faith and the Church. Obviously, theology can be developed both in dynamic times and in peaceful times, but what is necessary for its development is for the body of Christ to be full of life.

**Fr. Stamatis:** I can frankly say that I still have not fully understood what an icon actually is. Maybe it is not possible to either fully understand or express it. It is a great spiritual and pictorial mystery. However, I truly believe that the Byzantine icon is the most superb theological language expressed through colors, a language capable of truly expressing salvific dogmas. The icon is so profound because it conveys everything; even its tiniest detail conveys the entire theological truth. Nevertheless, we could not say that, besides the Byzantine icon, there are no other valuable pictorial expressions of the Christian faith, or that we could demand that absolutely everyone should paint in the manner of Byzantine icon painting. The Byzantine icon is certainly the most superb pictorial expression of the Christian faith, but we should be open minded and open to the idea that in the future other Christian people, if they lived the Orthodox faith in an authentic way, will be able to find equally valuable pictorial and iconographic expressions and solutions.

### 13. What is the role of prayer in the art of icon painting?

**Fr. Stamatis:** Prayer unites us in an existential bond with the Triune God. We should be careful not to perceive prayer in a pan-religious way, but in an authentically Orthodox way. That means liturgically

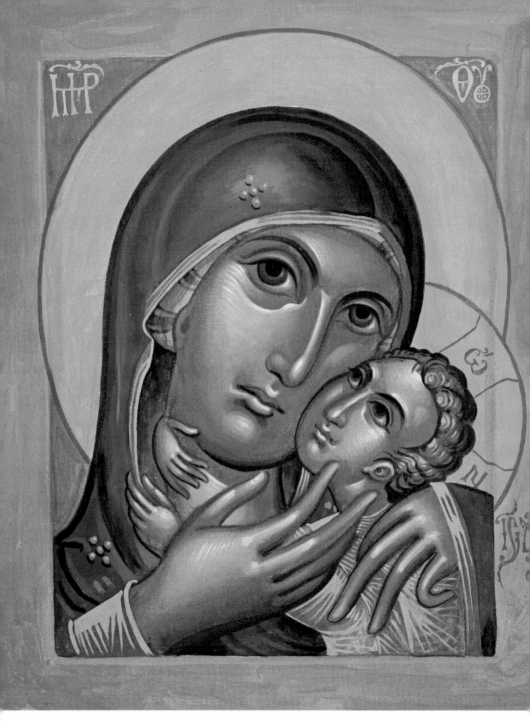

*Stamatis Skliris*
**Most Holy Theotokos,**
egg tempera on wooden board, 2007

and eucharistically. Prayer is not seclusion, which would allow me to remember psychologically those whom I love and for whom I pray, but it is, if we see it in a eucharistic way, foremost a practice, an act, which includes corporality and the material human side even though it has a spiritual dimension. Liturgy is, above all, an act of the people and not of individual self-consciousness. Prayer in liturgy indicates that and leads into many becoming One. In relation to icon painting, the very act of painting Christ or a saint is an act of prayer. The icon painter forms a bridge between God and man by painting; he unites the created with the Uncreated, and he does so by offering his piece of work, his theological expression through colors, as a gift to the liturgical community of the Church.

**Fr. Marko:** Prayer is the essence of the creation of ecclesiastical art. It means synergy between man and the Holy Spirit who prays for us. Prayer means comprehension and discernment of our relationship with the God the Father. This relationship with God is attainable for us only in Jesus Christ. The only one which moves people in the direction of God is the Holy Spirit. He that makes us children in the Son and through the incessant call of "Abba!" makes us true children.

That means that true prayer is an art of togetherness. That is why, as Macarius the Great teaches us, true prayer comes from a combination of our effort and grace. Prayer and grace are inseparable; their common denominator is the Holy Spirit. This is exactly my experience; we pray as persons together in the liturgy and we cooperate in an artistic act for the Church. It is not possible to create for churches if that does not come from the Church. The greatest ascetism is mercy, certainly. It would be even simpler to listen to the psalms while painting, pray while making a mosaic, but certainly the true test of faith is in the possibility of living together and in mutual collaboration. It is not enough to confess Christ orally and to pray orally, but we must witness to Christ, confirm His redemption, that is, actualize His love: "Everyone who loves has been born of God and knows God. Whoever does not love does not know God, because God is love... No one has ever seen God; but if we love one another, God lives in us and his love is made complete in us... Whoever lives in love lives in God, and God in him." These words of St. John bring forth what is important for a Christian artist. Objects, figures should be painted the way God sees them, as they are redeemed by Him, sanctified by Him. Knowledge of God is fulfilled in love. It is so easy to fool oneself with ideas of one's own or to feel strong and confident with learned doctrines, if all of that is seperated from ecclesiastical practice, from love. We could be exquisite artists, capable of doing many things, but until these works are living, inhabited by the Presence, the intervention of the Holy Spirit is needed. On our behalf, the only assurance is that we are open to God and that He can pass through us and our works and that our prayer is joined with grace.

If we are in unity, God creates in us and our art is a true notion and expression of the Church. In my humble experience over the years, I have seen that this is the most powerful spiritual experience, which is then translated into creativity. It is obvious that the life of prayer, the contemplation of the mystery of faith, and spiritual unity create the conditions for an artist's personal life, which enables the creation of liturgical art. My experience in Centro Aletti's Atelier is proof to me that a great sensibility for authentic spiritual art exists today, an art that is ecclesiastical and theologically profound. Our team of artists combines eight different nations and four different confessions.

## 14. What is "artistic inspiration" in your opinion?

**Fr. Marko:** In artistic creation, inspiration is the smallest part that is actually a condition without which a work of art remains sterile. A big part of it lies in work and in spiritual study. One should always have a vigorous heart with theological questions. It should be fed daily with spiritual thoughts and the Scripture. One should read the Church Fathers, the saints, Scripture, and observe the works of great Christian eras. At the same time, one should keep in mind what our contemporaries are exploring and creating. Christ, the apostles, and the Church Fathers never lost contact with people, with the world. One has to learn how to be in this world and not of this world. While studying, reading, meditating, one should maintain a conversation with God through prayer, know how to interrupt God, suggest to Him one's intuitions and observe His reaction.

The goal of studying consists, fundamentally, of two points. The first is entry into the dimension of memory, overcoming loneliness and the risk of self-delusion. A master that works on real initial memory and tradition is always needed. The other element of

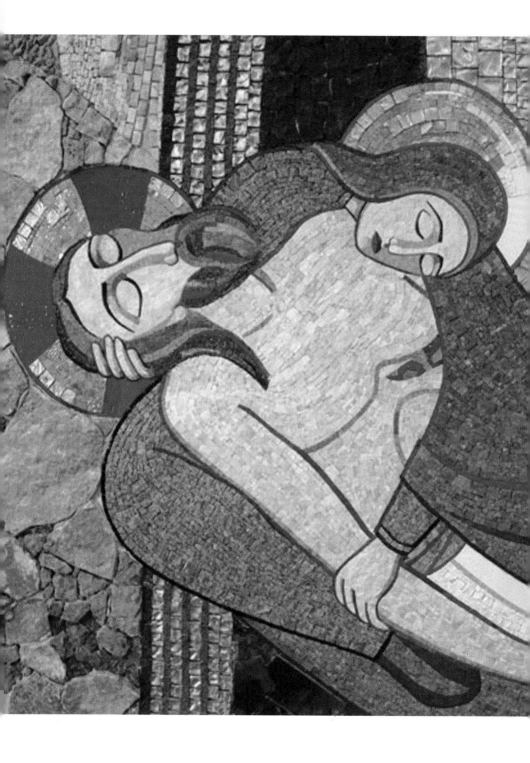

studying is in being humble. The objective of
studying is to obtain humility and obedience. All of
that should be placed in a relationship of love
between God and the artist. The tenet of all creativity
is a calling – to feel summoned, lured, enchanted by
the mystery of God's love, by the Holy Trinity itself.
The artist must let himself be drawn in; he must head
toward the voice that is calling him. Through study
and research, a moment is reached when an artist
realizes he is not the one who is supposed to ascend
to reach knowledge; instead, God descends and
looks for him and wants to communicate with him.
In my opinion, the most important moment is when
the artist, under the aegis of Church, in ecclesiastical
unity, in an intimate dialogue with God, draws
himself up, places himself in front of God, wants to
put himself at His disposal, makes space. Then God
starts to reveal Himself. It could be months of work,
research, prayer, asceticism, meetings, conversations
with different people, and then suddenly the artist
prostrates himself and the Holy Spirit is telling him
everything. Images pour into his heart and his eyes
accept them. The composition forms, details
disappear. Then, the endeavor of surrendering the
body to that whole realization begins. It is a test to
see if it communicates with others. It is a practice of
considering others, forming a real communication.
In this manner, we can re-enter memory and
tradition through a fertile dialogue with our world
today. Inspiration has only one source—the Holy
Spirit. He can reach our hearts through many things;
the most important is that we are humble, because
the gift is given to the humble, and denied to the
defiant, and to be in the community because He can

*Marko Rupnik*
Detail: **Repose of the
Mother and the Son
Capitel Hall,**
Cathedral Santa
Maria la Real
de La Almudena,
Madrid – Spain,
October 2006

be recognized only among others, in unity with the Church.

The liturgy and sacraments, foremost, teach us to go forward by remembering. We advance by making memory of what is, we become what we remember that is. Without a rich memory, inspiration is frail.

**Fr. Stamatis:** What inspires me are the great masters of the 14th century, anonymous ones; Serbian medieval painting, Sopocani foremost, then Giacometti and Picasso. Among modern Greek painters, Tsarouchis. However, most often, unpredictable things arouse my sensitivity, a flower or a beautiful color that I use to paint the robe of St. Marina.

Artistic inspiration is not found and sought in everyday life. Except in those rare moments, in moments of creativity. And they do not express an artist's skillfulness, but his sensitivity.

*15. Who are your artistic role models?*

**Fr. Stamatis:** I have one model that I use in painting. It is a gaze of a man who has fallen deeply into sin, and, while he is looking at me, an existential earthquake is taking place inside him. He yearns for forgiveness, for holiness, for union with the community of the Holy Ones and with God. There is not a better source for icon painting than this desire of a fallen man for redemption, for perfection, for the divine and holy.

**Fr. Marko:** Since Pope John Paul II gave me a job in his Capella Redemptoris Mater (Chapel of the Redeemer's Mother), I embarked on a intensely spiritual, artistic, and theological road. The image of the artist I strive for is in the workshops of the first millennium and of the Middle Ages where artists gathered around one artist made a group, a real social artistic workshop where art was being made on ecclesiological principles. It can be said that the workshop is a place for achieving life in unity, liturgy and life, but also a place for searching, for dialogues and experiments. In my opinion, the mosaic was so strongly accepted by the Church for at least two reasons, which I want to see as gradually coming closer to the ideals of schools and workshops of the first millennium. First, because it is certain that the mosaic expresses in a concrete way the synthesis of the dogma of creation and redemption. Saint Maximus the Confessor has synthesized the Holy Fathers' theology of creation by saying the world is created by the Logos Who left His mark, His code in the created. The Logos could be interwoven as an orientation, as a hierarchy of things, as a hierarchical order and therefore, the Logos means a direction of the world, an orientation the world wants to take. St. Maximus says the created wants to choose the path of Resurrection, which leads to life without sunset, the only reality without sunset being the love God gives through the intercession of the Holy Spirit. The created would like to come in and be a part of that love. That love is given in a special way only to man, as a person that is created in God's image. Man's body is a receptacle of the Holy Spirit, which gives love, and has the possibility to become embraced in that love, to put itself in the service of love and thus be imbued by love and drawn into it. Everything that is drawn into love is cut off from death for the sake

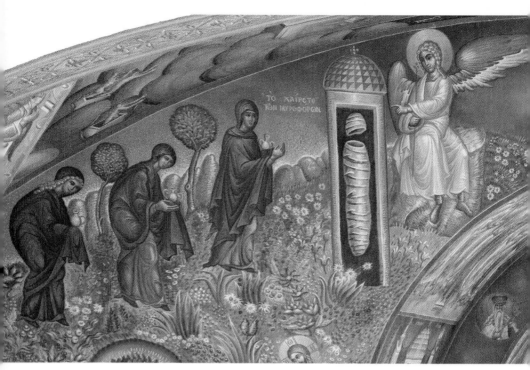

*Stamatis Skliris*
**Appearance of the Lord to the Holy Myrrhbearing Women**,
acrylic on wall,
St Nectarius Church, Voula – Greece, 2009

of resurrection, because love lasts forever and knows no boundaries. The created would like to be a part of that path, because the will of that which was created according to the Logos is to become a gift in hands of men. The created want to become a gift we as people give to each other, but when matter becomes imbued with love, it becomes a body. And when a body is a conscious carrier of love, consciously in service of love, it concentrates itself on the person. Because love always has a face. Love is the maximal realization and expression of an individual. That is why matter wants to acquire a face, because it wants to be imbued with love and to live in it. The mosaic stresses exactly this. A stone, a raw matter of the world, is arranged in a manner that it becomes a body and an image. This is even more possible after the avant-gardes of the twentieth century, because modern art has achieved significant results in everything related to matter, form, and movement. Besides that, it has demonstrated that material and color are two autonomous languages of art. This allows life to be seen, above all the life of the Spirit, which reveals itself in the created and through the created. Another element is the element of community, ecclesiality. A mosaic isn't individual, but a joint work. If a work is joint, it can only have one model, and that is of the Church. The Church model does not mean starting with abstract principles, from abstract rules and unchangeable projects. It means starting with the principle of agape, one that is subject to others. That is why the same space, the same workshop becomes a miniature of the Church, a little Church where we experiment with catholicity, symphony, and synergy. By making a mosaic we become a mosaic. Everyone has their place in relation to others, and in relation to the work that is being done. In this objective world of legalists and moralists, this is a true revolution for the world, but in a sense for the Church too, because a lot is being said about collegiality, catholicity, and personalism, but with no real experience. So the models and paintings of masters that I strive for are those of the ancient Church and Church Fathers.

*16. In your opinion, what are the essential aesthetic categories of Christian painting? Which one dominates your painting?*

**Fr. Marko**: From early Christian art until day, there have been three inseparable dimensions of Christian art. One of those is the dimension of realism: artistic painting obeys reality, it is tied to the real world;. Then, there is the dimension of the idea that the work of art contains: a work of art possesses a message that could be tied to a theological idea or the idea of revelation. The third dimension, which stems from the first two, is a symbol: i.e. the work is present and communicative. On a formal level, it is intended as an essential representation, with a certain "lens" of senses for details that could be rich, enchanting and attractive for the senses, but would cause confusion in these three aforementioned dimensions. That is why a painting is created with a concern for the essential, even though some moments in Christian art may seem childish. But that is precisely exactly its main strength: lines, facial expressions, looks must be clear, without anything distractive. The proportions and composition are not based on scientific rules, but on spiritual content and theology. The mentality and rules of the creation of the eighth day are the criteria for composing scenes, episodes, and sights in works of art. As for the colors, we choose strong and bright ones.

Bright color represents individuality and the Christian faith that recognizes the undistorted unity of personality. The triune principle of agape expresses the strength of unity without persons conforming to chance in order to be together. Harmony, the symphony of free individuals, is the real ecclesiastical art, which is based on the union of the Trinity. This is also the aesthetic principle of Christian art. The light does not shine from without but transpires from within.

That is the canon that is based on the theology of creation and pneumatology. Light and life are inseparable in the Bible and that is why Christian art must show movement and dynamic, which are the effects of light that is life. The mosaic, as we understand it and create it in our workshop, takes a lot of its creativity from this canon on the use of light.

**Fr. Stamatis:** As for my painting, I would not say that I wish to follow one specific tenet or one particular school. What typifies my painting is an attempt to exhibit man and the nature that surrounds him in a new light, in the new dimension that the God-Man and Savior introduced into our existence. That is, it is an attempt to describe with colors, lines, and everything else that is used in pictorial expression something in the created's existence that is ontologically new and that reflects the Incarnation of the Son of God and His

69

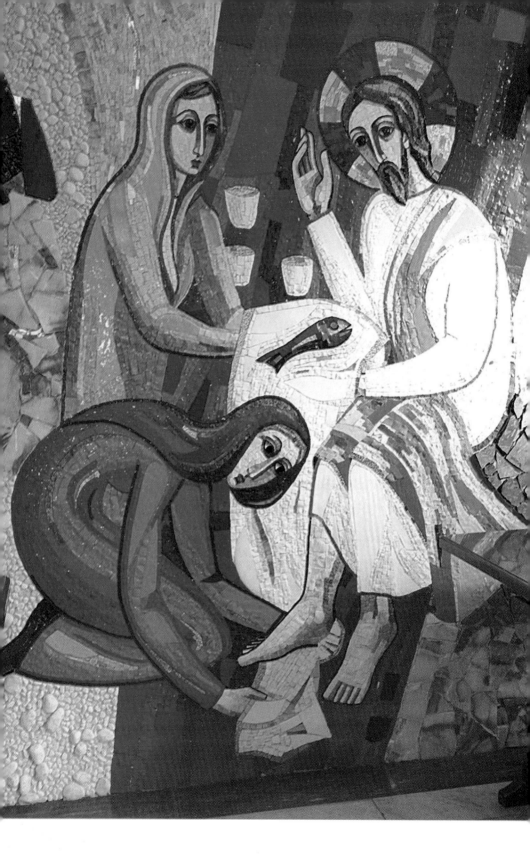

Resurrection from the dead. It is an attempt to display all these events as events that took place in history for us, for each one of us individually, and that we are called upon to participate in these events. Further, the specific space in which our participation is realized is the space of our Church and her Eucharistic service, which constitutes us as a community, not just a community of religious people, but as the Body of Christ Himself. And what is very important for icon painting is that it testifies that the process of the transformation of man and the entire creation has already begun, here in real time, and the heralds and best witnesses of this are our saints. For this reason it is important for icon painting not to perceive history in its factuality, not to view it in a way that binds it to the limits of its historicity, because it already carries within itself a token of the transformation to come. This token, of course, is the existence of the Church in the world in the form of its liturgical gathering.

### 17. What do you consider to be the crucial differences between icon painting in Roman Catholicism and the Orthodox Church?

**Fr. Stamatis:** Western painting is, in my opinion, placed more within history, while Eastern painting focuses more on a vision of the future. Western painting strives for depicting natural space and time, while Eastern painting has developed a rhythm that creates a sense of the transfiguration of these realities, overcoming the natural impression of the world. As for its function, Western art, in perceiving the relationship between God and man, emphasizes the didactic and ethical dimensions of this relationship.

*Marko Rupnik*
**Anointing in Bethany,**
Centro Aletti,
Rome – Italy,
October 2002

71

Eastern painting is centered more on the liturgical, sacramental experience and tries to reveal and convey a vision of the world that is to come. As for the ethos, Western painting practices, to a certain extent, theatrical expression. In presenting events from the past, it insists on dramatizing. It should be acknowledged that both painting traditions are in many elements indebted to old Greek drama. An icon painter, regardless of the tradition, must know how to direct a scene with multiple participants in an actual event. Also, he must be aware that he is directing a space that is immediately concerned with realities that touch on our existential leanings in a most profound way. In Western painting, a desire to highlight a notion of fullness and richness, which is achieved by emphasizing certain architectural or costume details, can often be discerned. Eastern painting, on the other hand, like a sort of pantomime and with very few words, tries to send a message with eschatological content. Briefly put, in the theological sense, Eastern painting is more inspired by the Resurrection, and Western, it seems, more by the Cross and Passion of our Lord.

**Fr. Marko**: In my opinion, there is no significant difference between painting in the Catholic Church and painting in the Orthodox Church. One who would like to see these significant differences would have to find significant differences in the dogma concerning Christ. And it would only be possible to do such a thing if one were ignorant of theology. There are differences in languages, approaches, emphases, but even these differences decrease or increase depending on time and place. The Catholic Church includes a broad spectrum of peoples and, because of that, the presence of different cultures is accentuated. However, this is only an impetus to the greater celebration of colors and not an obstacle that stresses the importance of differences. For the one who feels close to Christ, difference means wealth, because union with Christ does not collide with something else. He who stands far from Christ senses difference as a curse. To me, the only interesting thing today is the exchange of ideas, as I mentioned before. I am a Roman Catholic, a Jesuit; I studied theology, and eight years of Orthodox theology. Moreover, I have continued doing so in the past years. I have read nothing about Orthodoxy out of curiosity, or from desire for comparative studies, but simply from a desire for better faith, better theological thinking, because everything that is Christ's is also mine. I am Slovenian, but I feel Catherine of Siena as my own, St. Francis as my own, but also Andrei Rublov and St. Sava. A Russian monk once told me: "Very nice, I cannot get angry with you or yell at you, because if I do so I will show you that those things of ours that you consider to be yours because they are Christ's are not actually from Christ if I don't allow them to be yours also."

## 18. Does the spirit of Post-Modernism add to the revitalization of Christian art?

**Fr. Marko**: In today's world, we don't know what's postmodern. However, what is usually considered postmodern is a reality that is truly eclectic. For example, something typically postmodern is a fragility of identity, hence the need for a blind and mindless attack on tradition and rules. Something typically postmodern is a call for religion without

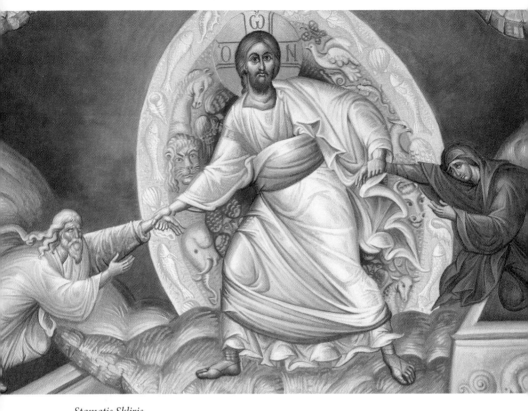

*Stamatis Skliris*
**Resurrection (detail),**
acrylic on wall,
St Nectarius Church, Voula – Greece, 2009

any affiliation. It's an affirmation of nationality without any cognizance and with a minimal amount of cultured behavior. But these demands seem violent and are made with an energy that replaces competence and experience. Something typically modernist is to want strong regimes, obedience to the rules that are experienced, with lots of room for subjective freedom. One can often find people with some knowledge of rules of faith, iconography, but living as completely immersed in modern consumerism. For the latter, Dahrendorf says it is typical for this transitional phase. Also characteristic of postmodernism is a blurry climate of vagueness, indefiniteness, and compensation for memory, tradition, but with no involvement and impetus. I do not know if it could be said that postmodernism itself is reviving Christian art. I think that the fact that postmodernism is relativistic toward the scientific, philosophical, and political dogmatism of modernity creates suitable atmosphere for creativity. Today, we could call it time without wind. The only way to move a boat is by rowing. That is why I would dare to say that these last ten years have been ten years of testing vitality, and seeing who has the strength and will to row. It is not time for protests, lamentation, and tears. One who is doing that in these years is only losing. Therefore, the history of southeast Europe has something to say about that, too. Now is the time of those who create, who have vital, creative, and inventive strength. The greatest favor of the postmodern climate to us Christians is the possibility of opinion* with suggestions.

---

* Attitude, stance

75

**Fr. Stamatis**: Postmodernism has a positive aspect for us Orthodox Christians. It re-examines old cultural models. In this context, it allows us to reappraise even Byzantine painting, that is the icon, whose meaning we Christians and people outside Church, too, may have forgotten in some sense. In this light, the appearance of a theology of the icon, which did not exist in the era in which the icon was made in Byzantium, is understandable. The theology of the icon is a modern phenomenon that testifies to the fact that there are uncertainties regarding to this topic. Postmodernism has, on the other hand, a negative element because in some parts it connects external forms and elements of various cultures of the past, creating a new form of art that loses its intrinsic functionality. All the elements that made it into this new artistic form primarily had functionality because they emanated from the experience of people living in specific cultures. In the case of postmodernism, we have a new form made out of different cultural elements as a creation that emanated only from the mind of artist. It did not emanate from real life. For example, in a painting, an artist can take eyes from a Byzantine Virgin Mary and unite them with a Chinese element. In architecture, he can take a dome and connect it to a pagoda. But those who are going to enter that building or live in it are neither going to be Byzantine Christians who piously enter a domed shrine, nor Eastern mystics entering a pagoda. This building does not belong to life organically, but only aesthetically. Therefore, this is about an aesthetic separated from life.

Hence, an icon—viewed as an artistic creation that transcends time, which draws its life from the faithful entering the church to venerate it, viewed as a very unique form of painting that the faithful kiss and respect as if it were a living and present person—cannot be turned into a postmodern type of art. The function of the icon is that when it is placed inside a sanctuary it represents the living presence of the transfigured world within the space of the Holy Eucharist. However, apart from all that, I think that to me, personally, postmodernism contributed something very important. What is that? It taught me a very fruitful practice: to combine things that at first glance seem impossible to connect, in such a way that a synthesis is made between them. An approach like that in the moment when an icon is being painted assumes that Tradition is not perceived as a self-explanatory reality. Therefore, what we have here is a somewhat problematic practice that can endanger Tradition. However, in my case, it elicited the realization that even Tradition can be dangerous if it teaches me only to accept readymade solutions, if it teaches me only, for example, to imitate my elder in a superficial way or to imitate, let's say, Panselinos and formal features of his painting. In that case, it would lead me to spiritual and iconographic decline. While I was painting the Virgin Platytera (More Spacious than the Heavens) with Athanasius Koutzipetzidis in the church of St. Nectarius in Voula, we painted the enthroned Virgin in a very conservative and traditional way and Christ in a postmodern, so to speak. He has the expression of a very strong child and his dress is painted in an impressionist manner.

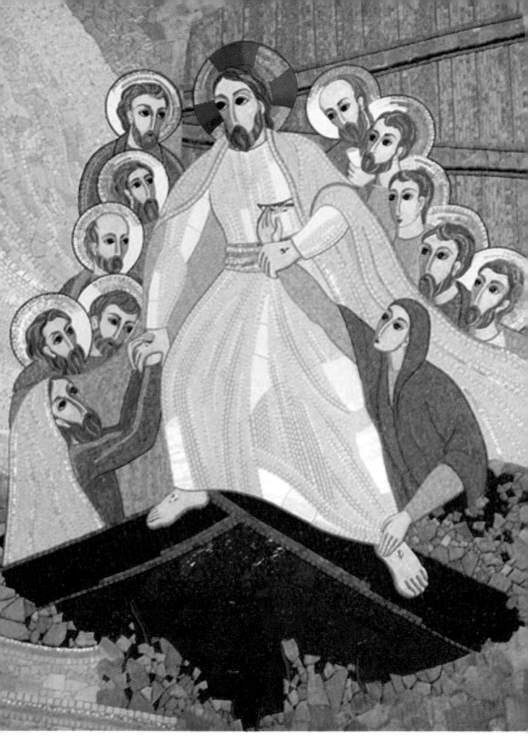

*Marko Rupnik*
**The Descent into Hades in the Composition of the Risen Jesus,**
Chapel at Sacred Heart University, Fairfield, Connecticut – USA, August 2008

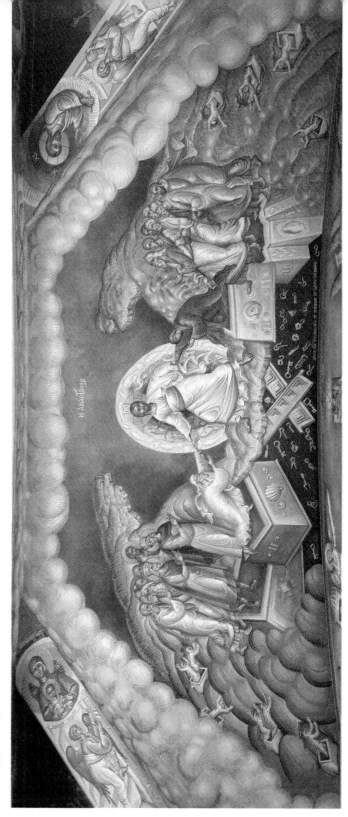

*Stamatis Skliris*
**Resurrection,
acrylic on wall,**
St Nectarius Church,
Voula – Greece, 2009

The synthesis of a Byzantine Virgin and impressionist elements is, we could say, in a broader sense, a postmodern practice. And this is its significance: that within the arms of a solemn mother, the Theotokos, appears a divine child who keeps inside of him all the strength of divinity, and, what is of particular importance, expresses divine action in human history. I believe that the Theotokos is a vessel that serves to incorporate the God-Man Christ into the community of men.

### 19. How do you see the role of the icon in a "cyber universe"?

**Fr. Stamatis:** To properly evaluate the problems that arise from this question, Metropolitan John of Pergamon suggests that the criterion must be the body and the participation of the body in the context of human activity. We should, therefore, first of all see how an ecclesiastical icon perceives corporeality and how a cyber icon or image sees it. The correct answer to the question comes from how accurately we understand the concept of corporeality in both cases. Following that, we should connect personality with corporeality. Finally, we move to the question of comparing the comic strips and the icon. Icons on which we paint saints with a body that has no fullness, as in the case of, let's say, Coptic icons, lead us to the impersonal characters that we see in comic strips. Icons on which the saint is an actual person with an actual body, thus corporal, express most fully the Orthodox conception of the icon in general sense, hence in the sense of Tradition. By trying to answer this question, we come to the subject of why it is imperative that icons have plasticity, to express space, three dimensions with some reversed perspective, but always to express body with dimension, and not just some abstract vision. Icons are, in fact, visions; that is, they express visions, but, at the same time, they are representations with concrete historical content that always includes corporeality. In the context of corporeality, an unavoidable factor is also the materiality of the icon. An icon which is correctly painted and which can rightly participate in the Divine Liturgy is only an icon that is made of matter, wood, or anything else, and with material colors and which is done by an icon painter.

Thus we come to the question of printed icons, ones that were done by machines and not by men. In cyber space, however, we do not even have machines which, we could say, represent material elements, but instead, we have an absence of the corporal in general. It has become possible for all human actions to be made without using the body – for instance, to go somewhere, to reach something, to connect with other people, to buy something, and so on. The further problem is that those actions, those products of cyberspace, are reproductions, they could be reproduced innumerable times and remain identical. Such a phenomenon—for there to be two completely identical things – never before existed in human life; even two leaves from a single tree, for instance, are different. All that is obliterated now, because digitally it is possible to make things exactly the same. According to Metropolitan John of Pergamon, this is something monstrous from the perspective of the sense of the uniqueness of the person, because this phenomenon introduces a new mentality of generalization and an attitude to life that consents to the loss of uniqueness and the fact that the person does not use his corporeality. That is why we could say, in response to your question, that the Orthodox stance is very reserved toward icons in cyberspace. Even though we are forced to use means that come from the so-called cyberspace, because life has reached a stage where it is impossible to avoid it, where it is impossible to work without using these means, we are still concerned about it, to say the least. However, the topic raised by this question is so big that it requires not just one, but many studies, and therefore what we have said is only a kind of first reaction based on an experience of the Orthodox understanding of reality in general.

**Fr. Marko**: Cyber art is characterized by a powerful and meticulous mentality of dealing with complexity, a complexity of messages and language. It is a product on the border between a scientific modernist mentality and new virtual entertainment technology. I think that to Christians, if they are truly spiritual, everything is permitted; still, we could never unite with cyber and virtual art completely. We believe, not in a mentality of mathematics, but in a mentality of community and agape. For us, there is no universal plan, strict and totalitarian, but a Father who is merciful and faithful. Ours is a faith of incarnation, and that is why nothing that is made of abstract principles and that wants to rule history can be accepted. The role of icon in this world is certainly great and fundamental, even though, like all painting, it has a certain amount of allusion and pretense (because of its two-dimensional surface). In some sense, I think that working with stone, in mosaic, can be a greater challenge to cyber and virtual culture, because stone teaches us to consider it. This is learned, if not in any other way, then, by cutting it. Because if you do not seriously consider it and you want to cut it, you will see that you will cut yourself, but you will not cut the stone. It's one thing to break a stone, and another to cut it. Under a knowing and careful blow, a stone is opened. The problem with cyber world is objectivity, because in fact, the imaginary has a greater value than existing objectivity. But the objective power of the icon is the Church, with its tradition, aesthetic, liturgy, its language and canons. In that sense, I see that the icon can help in leading a man to something he must admit himself exists and which is not just a product of his that he can manipulate in any way he likes.

*20. Ecumenical dialogue is more intensive. Great efforts are being made to establish once again unity in the Christian world. To what extent can ecclesiastical art contribute to that?*

**Fr. Marko**: Ecumenism is the path of all Christians, the path of everyone who has been baptized, especially in the Churches with apostolic tradition. Chapter seventeen of the Gospel according to John cannot be less important than any other chapter in the Gospels. In this chapter, Christ does not give any space for dilemma or subjective interpretations: community is necessary for us to call ourselves Christians. The history that we have created will lead us to ruins if we do not confess our sin of schism. I think that art is a privileged place where we

Christians can testify together that our love for Christ is more powerful than our schism. In countries in which Christianity has disappeared or is disappearing, what is left are only testimonies of saints, martyrs, and works of Christian art. The Metropolitan of Cluj, Bartolomeu Anania, said, when blessing the beginning of our work in his church, that this is not just regular ecumenism, but true togetherness of the Churches. Liturgical art, because it reveals the truth – that is, what truly exists – confesses communication between the Churches, because that communication is already fulfilled in Christ. It is not an abstract or artificial discussion, but the matter of how to create something beautiful for Christ, for the Church and the believers. Future generations will judge our generation very severely, which, after decades and centuries, had a great chance to do something together, but it seems we are not capable of doing that. This could mean that our love for the beautiful – that is, for God's fulfilled love – has grown cold and it has grown cold because we do not have a taste of that love. Wherever we Christians have the opportunity to create together by constructing a church that is beautiful, theologically rich, and empowered by the presence of God's sanctity, we are obliged to do everything in our power to respond to the call of God. We often criticize the European Union; we make judgments about a union that is based on economics and finance. But it should be said that it is exactly us Christians who have given Europe into the hands of neo-paganism, aggressive Islam, and "populations" yet to come, since we, torn and separated and fanatics of our own misery could not have nor could we be the yeast of unity for our continent.

**Fr. Stamatis**: The unity of the Church is the most significant question. For every problem that is concerned with the question of unity, we should care about it deeply and fight fiercely to overcome it with God's help, and of course, through dialogue. Certainly, in the present circumstances, the realization of unity seems very difficult, requiring lots of time, above all, because of human weakness and passion. Concerning the icon, I am under the impression that there has been a rapprochement between the Catholics, the Anglicans, and the Orthodox in understanding the gravity, sanctity, and theology that is expressed by a Byzantine icon. We call the Byzantine icon an Orthodox icon, but we would not mind if the non-Orthodox perceived it as their own, and therefore, we will not call it an Orthodox icon, but with a broader name, that is more common anyway – a Byzantine icon. Friends of mine, clerics of the Roman Catholic Church in Bologna, told me that when they are praying they abandoned Raphael's Madonna and they pray only before icons painted according to the Eastern tradition. They keep Raphael's Madonna only as paintings in their homes, but not in areas for praying. Many shrines, both Catholic and Anglican, keep Byzantine icons now. I do not have information concerning the rest of the Protestant world, but probably things are moving toward rapprochement, toward concordance on this topic. This may mean that the icon, because it represents highly complex, subtle theological language, from which every detail of the dogmatic teaching of the Church can be read, which naturally expresses love for Christ and love among men, speaks to every person, regardless of their confession. We should accept, without fear, that the art of painting does not possess the clarity and precision of theological language. Therefore, it is possible to find in an icon the elements that we described, but when we try to develop it through language, dogmatic language especially, we find differences. In any case, when it comes to an icon, we can all agree that we have a representation of Christ, iconized, presented in such a way that it shows that He has one hypostasis and two natures. On an icon, Personality is iconized; one and undivided Personality of the Word of God, Word Incarnated.

*Finally, we would like to thank Fr. Radovan Bigovic for the questions, which were really timely and stimulating, and which brought up so many issues that a whole book, at least, could have been devoted to them.*

# The Icon, the Kingdom, and the Hope for the World

We live in times awash with man-made images, in a postmodern epoch where each person struggles to produce the most convincing image of himself and his idea, where people fashion a self image to attract others, impressing and imposing with their "icon" or, better yet, their "idol" (as St Andrew says: "αὐτείδωλον ἐγενόμην", "I have become an idol to myself"; Canon of St. Andrew of Crete, Ode IV). It is an era that offers falsehood, delusion, and fantasy without transcending the antinomies and limitations of history.

We live in such times; yet, the two iconographers, Fr. Stamatis Skliris and Fr. Marko Rupnik, propose a transcendent alternative: one Divinely-revealed rather than human-made, one that is convicting rather than convincing, one that is iconic rather than idolatrous – the Icon of God.

This Icon represents humanity having received the opportunity to circumscribe and depict the Transcendent God, which only became possible once God became man, expressing his Divinity in human form, bringing the Kingdom of God into the Divine Liturgy, and demonstrating the reality of the Resurrection by asking one of His disciples to verify what he saw by touching Christ's hands, feet, and side (Jn 20:26). Similarly, the language of the Fathers about Icons, especially that of the Seventh Ecumenical Council, has to do with both seeing and beholding the vision of God. But this language introduces significant questions: What is the real image of God? What is the real image of man? What is the real image of this world? Does the Icon depict a Platonic ideal? Or does it represent Greco-Roman art? Or does the iconic image capture the corrupted world of Pieter Brueghel or Salvador Dali? Maybe, we Christians present an image that itself can obscure the image of the Kingdom? Do we not, instead of iconicizing the transfigured world of Paradise, most often represent the mere fallen world? This problem faces us in our present-day Church and it is necessary to ask ourselves: does our image of the world and the Church overshadow the true image of the Kingdom?

To answer this question, it is important that we understand the difference between the Icon and the image, between the Divine Image and the image of this world. The two, as Stamatis and Rupnik show so vividly, are altogether different.

The first, and significant, difference is that the Icon is not naturalistic; it does not represent something ephemeral, but rather it represents both a Person and a personal relationship. One of the most significant points to emerge from the Seventh Ecumenical Council is that one Divine Person – the Son of God – became man, demonstrating that we cannot speak about God or imagine God without the Person who revealed God to us. An image that does not refer to the Person of Christ is an image that refers to the corrupted world and thus leads to death. The Icon is not of this world; it is eschatological both in origin and in content. Not being drawn from history, we can call the Icon meta-historical.

Nevertheless, the Kingdom can only be depicted through created means. The Icon is distinct from the truth, not because it is false, delusional, or fantastic, but because it borrows its means of expression from still-corruptible nature.

Although its means of expression derive from fallen nature, the Icon refers to inexpressible Truth by encouraging our personal relations with Truth; a proper Icon creates true personal relationships. That is why an Icon is indivisibly linked with Love: we cannot speak about Truth without Love, and we cannot speak about an Icon that does not lead us to Love.

For Orthodox Christians, this means that the Icon leads us to the Church, where we meet the other in his or her true state. As St. Justin of Celie used to say, "in the Church we are taught to see (iconically) in every man our future brother/sister [as he or she is in] Paradise." There, in the Eucharistic synaxis, we will see and meet God through our communion with others. The Icon gathers (*synaxis*) the community we call the Church; it is not only an object that we kiss and venerate, but an eternal synaxis that exists in moments, movements, and actions during the Divine Liturgy. Outside the Church, there is not the Kingdom of God; inside the Church, all is iconic. Within the Church, we enter into a reality that Fr Rupnik identifies as "symbolic." "It is symbolic in its authentic theological meaning."

The Icon's theological meaning illuminates the next characteristic of the Icon: it refers to another, not to itself, leading us, thereby, out of solipsism. It encourages us to go out and meet the other. The Icon is person-oriented! When we venerate an Icon of Christ or a Saint, we demonstrate our victory over individualism and show that we are not self-reliant. When the Icon traces this relationship between persons (God and man) and gathers the Church, then the Church becomes a real depiction of the Kingdom of God, leading us to the Divine Eucharist, which St. Maximus the Confessor describes as the image or Icon of the Kingdom. In the primitive phase of the ancient Church, the Icon was closely linked with the mystery of the Eucharist. The Eucharist is the celebration that makes the earthly Church what it is, namely, an *Icon* of the Kingdom.

But, there is yet one more difference between the Icon and the image. The image "fixes" reality, as opposed to the Icon, which does not fix reality but liberates it from natural laws. We celebrate today the Fathers of the Seventh Ecumenical synod who gathered to testify that the Church could not exist without Icons, without iconicizing the Person of God! When an image becomes an Icon, it no longer refers to itself anymore – to its ephemeral existence; rather, it refers beyond itself: to that which exists beyond this corrupted world. When an image becomes an Icon, it redeems a person or landscape depicted in it and situates that person or landscape in relationship to the Kingdom. In the historical life of the Church, everything is an image of the future. The Icons which depict the Saints are not photographs of their historical faces, but the images of the future they portray.

This reality of the Icon's relationship with the Kingdom of Heaven is why the Fathers of the Seventh Ecumenical Council repeated what St. Basil said in the fourth century: "*the **honor** paid to the Icon passes on to the **prototype**"*! Therefore, when we venerate an Icon, that relationship goes beyond the Icon and reaches the Original source of the image, which is a Person. That is why in the Church, the Word is an Icon and an Icon is the Word! Our Church experiences this throughout the ages when it depicts and represents the Kingdom of God through Icons, through chanting, through harmonious architecture, and through all manner of aesthetic endeavors that are part of our Liturgical expression. The Orthodox survived under the Ottoman rule without catechism or schools only through this Iconic approach to embodying Truth. The pious people spoke with God through Icons (iconographic depictions) and Hymns and not through human words or rational formulations; God, in turn, revealed Himself to His people through Icons and Hymns.

This, in the final analysis, means, that the Divine worship in its liturgical-iconical context has saved the Orthodox Church and not the verbal descriptions and rhetoric of the homilists… such as this present one. The two dialogues suggest that the icon is the best and most authentic painterly expression of the Christian faith. That's why Fr Stamatis can say: "I truly believe that the Byzantine icon is the most superb theological language expressed through colors, a language capable of truly expressing salvific dogmas."

There will be those who challenge these dogmas, asserting that an iconic image conveys the Platonic idea of a shadow empty of reality. But such a position makes it difficult to speak of the Church as an Icon without falling into the realm of the imaginative or unreal. The Iconic nature of the Orthodox Church does not imply a lack of reality, although it does imply a lack of objectified and autonomous reality. As Metropolitan John of Pergamon states, "by being iconic in her existence the Church is two things: (a) she is an image of something else that transcends her—hence, again, a *relational* entity; and (b) she is in her institutions and structure so *transparent* as to allow the eschatological realities to be reflected in them all the time. This can hardly be achieved outside the context of worship, for it is there that transcendence and transparency are experienced par excellence."

In this society permeated with the *illusions of multimedia*, where image-pollution of all sorts has blurred our vision, we are invited to promote the true Icon of the Kingdom, we are invited to liberate our everyday life from slavery to the natural world through this iconical ethos that our Tradition bequeaths to us; an *iconological* ethos that leads to an affirmation of the other, which leads very often to "silence" and to deference before the other, who we prefer over ourselves ("Honor one another above yourselves" – Rom. 12:10).

Unfortunately, Orthodoxy in our times tends to become an ideology, wherein slogans and accusations of betraying the faith and tradition – understood ideologically – are hurled at one another. But, significantly enough, our Orthodox Church has chosen the commemoration of the Seventh Ecumenical Council to be *the* Sunday of Orthodoxy. As is well known, this Council dealt with the issue of Icons and did not put forth any propositional definition of the faith. In declaring, *"This is the faith of the Fathers; this is the faith which has sustained the oecumene,"* the Council pointed to a form of "theology," the Icon, which was the liturgical experience of the community and required no subscription to conceptual or ideological statements.

This declaration of the Seventh Council ended the Christological debate of words by testifying to the *reality of the Mystery* in the Icon of the Crucified and Risen Lord. This Icon removes our forgetfulness of the eschatological Coming of the Risen One, the eschatological Newness of the Living One (Rev. 1:17 and 21:5). Now "we call Christ's image 'Christ'... The Icon of Christ is nothing other than Christ, *apart, of course, from the difference in essence*" (St. Theodore the Studite).

The identification of the selfsameness of Christ with His image leads to our final point: Orthodox Christianity *is* the Church, *not* an ideology! It is a gathering of the people and, particularly, a Eucharistic gathering of living icons. This is what we must emphasize today; it is what Stamatis and Rupnik advocate when clarifying the role of the icon in a "cyber universe." We must not be satisfied with an Internet-accessible, online, virtual *illusion* of communication, but rather with the Icon as visible and true communication of the Kingdom; such *must* be the future of Christianity because such is the future Christ promises His Church. In the Eucharist, we are taught not only to venerate and greet icons, but also the other members of the synaxis, not passing the living icons – people – by, but greeting and embracing them. As the right method of looking at the world, the iconic approach will save Orthodoxy from becoming a secular organization conforming to *the image of the world*.

In these timely conversations led by Fr. Radovan Bigovic, many issues were introduced that enable the contemporary reader to deepen and expand his or her understanding of the role of art in the life of the Church. Here we find answers to questions on the crisis of contemporary ecclesiastical art in West and East; the impact of Impressionism, Expressionism, Cubism, Surrealism and Abstract painting on contemporary ecclesiastical painting; and a consideration of the main distinction between iconography and secular painting. The dialogues, while resolving some doubts about the difference between iconography, religious painting, and painting in general, reconciles the requirement to obey iconographic canons with the freedom essential to artistic creativity, demonstrating that obedience to the canons is not a threat to the vitality of iconography. Both artists illumine the role of prayer and asceticism in the art of iconography. They also metion crucial differences between iconography in the Orthodox Church and in Roman Catholicism. How important these distinctions are when exploring the relationship between contemporary theology and art! In a time when postmodern "metaphysics" relativizes every concept, these masters still believe that, to some extent, Post-Modernism adds to the revitalization of Christian art, stimulating questions about "artistic inspiration" and the essential aesthetic categories of Christian painting. Their exceptionally wide, yet nonetheless deep, expertise assists their not-so-everyday connections between theology, art, and modern issues concerning society – "society" taken in its broader meaning as "civilization." Finally, the entire artistic project of Stamatis and Rupnik has important ecumenical implications that answer a genuine longing for unity in the Christian world.

Bishop **Maxim** (Vasiljevic)
Western American Diocese

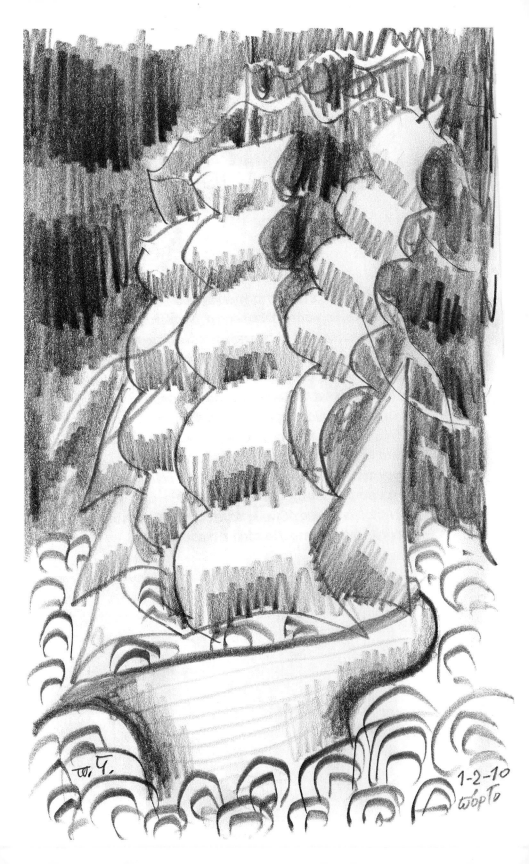